WOMAN
IN
SHARI'AH

WOMAN
IN
SHARI'AH
(Islamic Law)

'Abdul Rahman I. Doi

Published by
Ta-Ha Publishers Ltd
1, Wynne Road
London, S.W.9
United Kingdom

© Ta Ha Publishers Ltd. 1409 / 1989

Published by:
Ta-Ha PUBLISHERS Ltd.
1, Wynne Road
LONDON SW9 0BB, United Kingdom

1st Edition Published in Nigeria
2nd Edition Revised and edited by Abdalhaqq Bewley

British Library Cataloguing in Publication Data

Doi, A. Rahman I.
    Woman in Shari'a (2nd edition)
        1. Women - Legal status, Laws, etc.
    [Islamic Law]
I. Title
    340.5'9'088042 [Law]

ISBN 0-907461-60-3

Laser Typesetting by Bookwork, Norwich
Printed and bound in Great Britain at
The Camelot Press plc, Southampton

CONTENTS

PREFACE

When the wife of Imran said:
"My Lord I have vowed unto You
what is in my womb,
surely You are the One who knows and sees."
When she gave birth she said:
"I have given birth to a female child."
And Allah knew very well
what she had given birth to.
The male is not like the female.(3:35,36)

Allah has created man and woman to play distinct roles in human society and a woman's biology and physique best suit her, at base, for the maternal role so necessary in the creation of healthy and happy families.

Alexis Carrel, the French Nobel Laureate, rightly says[1] that the differences which exist between men and women are of a more fundamental nature than is usually realised and that these differences are caused by the very structure of the tissues and by the impregnation of the entire organism with specific chemical substances secreted by the ovary.

He continues: "Ignorance of these fundamental facts has led promoters of feminism to believe that both sexes should have the same responsibilities. In reality woman differs profoundly from man. Every one of the cells of her body bears the mark of her sex. The same is true of her organs and, above all, of her nervous system."[2] Women should, according to him, "develop their aptitudes without imitating the males." These aptitudes fall in the area of family, household, rearing of children and making a happy home.

Dr. Muhammad Abu Sa'ud has pointed out[3] that if a woman is given androgen (a male hormone) she becomes aggressive unless she is suffering from some societal trauma and if a violently aggressive man is given estrogen (a female hormone), in most cases he will calm down and start to behave in a docile manner.

He further says that if a transsexual individual chooses to

become a female by undergoing surgical intervention, estrogen hormone therapy is necessary to build up the breasts, to establish female sexual desires, to eliminate profuse facial and body hair etc. He has discovered that once the new female is given such hormonal stimulus the maternal instinct becomes intensely felt, the desire for talking becomes more persistent, feminine emotionality supercedes rationality, and the lachrymatory glands secrete more tears during emotional stress, all of which make up the natural characteristics of a woman.[4]

According to Weitz: "Animal evidence does support the concept of the maternal instinct, in that female sex hormones such as estrogen, progesterone, and prolactin seem to be implicated in the ontogeny of maternal behaviour."[5] Nowhere in the animal kingdom do fathers assume the basic role of caring for the newly born offspring. A monkey mother was no sooner given androgen (a male hormone) than it killed its newly born babies.[6]

It is, indeed, a natural phenomenon that a female child is born with a maternal instinct. She distinctly feels a strong interest in children, and this explains why girls prefer to play with dolls. Weitz has also shown that girls with an excess of androgen do seem to show less interest in infants than normal girls,[7] and obviously more than normal boys. Maternal behaviour is mainly characterised by tenderness, affective bonds, self-preservation, protectiveness and self-identification with the child.

According to Diamond a female is born with a maternal instinct carrying genetic dispositions different from those of a male.[8] It is also of interest to note that there is differential treatment of children according to their sex. Mothers are more inclined to tolerate boys than girls, while fathers are more tolerant towards girls than boys.

Dr. Alexis Carrel also feels that males and females have differences in the dispositions of their nerves and in their mental and emotional talents. "Partisans of women's liberation," says Dr. Carrel, "aim at a false conception of equality, as if that desirable condition meant a precise similarity and identity in upbringing, employment, responsibilities and duties."[9] Islam does not take such a lopsided view of human nature, but assigns those functions to men and women for which their respective natures are most suited.

Even the staunchest proponents of liberalism cannot deny that the male is created with more muscular strength than the female, that biologically speaking he is more 'aggressive', that his mind is more outwardly inclined, and that he is freer from cyclical physiological effects, and that the female is created with an innate predisposition for childbirth. It serves society's best interests if sex roles are assigned in accordance with natural aptitude and characteristics, and this is precisely what Islam does.

The Prophet (peace be upon him) strongly advised Muslim men and women to get married and bring harmonious families into existence. It is actually harmonious families that make a society well-knit and strong, free from imbalance and delinquency. Thus a woman's role in Islamic society is clearly, at base, to rear children and create a wholesome and happy home.

The duty of parents, therefore, is to give their daughters training from an early age to be prepared for marriage and childbirth. Ludovici says: "It seems eminently desirable to emphasise, more than we have emphasised in the past, the ideal of matrimony for every girl up to a certain age, and to bring home to parents that marriage is what they must train them for."[10]

Islam has thus made woman an honoured partner of man in raising a family. A chaste and virtuous woman is a blessing to her household, and makes her children virtuous in the way of Allah. Muslim women correctly appreciate this role laid down by Allah and His Messengers and take pride in fulfilling it.

1
WOMEN IN THE QUR'AN AND THE SUNNA

In Islam there is absolutely no difference between men and women as far as their relationship to Allah is concerned, as both are promised the same reward for good conduct and the same punishment for evil conduct. The Qur'an says:

> **And for women are rights over men**
> **similar to those of men over women. (2:226)**

The Qur'an, in addressing the believers, often uses the expression, **'believing men and women'** to emphasize the equality of men and women in regard to their respective duties, rights, virtues and merits. It says:

> **For Muslim men and women,**
> **for believing men and women,**
> **for devout men and women,**
> **for true men and women,**
> **for men and women who are patient and constant,**
> **for men and women who humble themselves,**
> **for men and women who give in charity,**
> **for men and women who fast,**
> **for men and women who guard their chastity,**
> **and for men and women**
> **who engage much in Allah's praise,**
> **for them has Allah prepared**
> **forgiveness and great reward. (33:35)**

This clearly contradicts the assertion of the Christian Fathers that women do not possess souls and that they will exist as sexless beings in the next life. The Qur'an says that women have souls in exactly the same way as men and will enter Paradise if they do good:

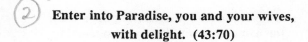

Enter into Paradise, you and your wives,
with delight. (43:70)

Whoso does that which is right, and believes,
whether male or female,
him or her will We quicken to happy life. (16:97)

The Qur'an admonishes those men who oppress or ill-treat women:

O you who believe! You are forbidden
to inherit women against their will.
Nor should you treat them with harshness,
that you may take away part of the dowry
you have given them - except when
they have become guilty of open lewdness.
On the contrary live with them
on a footing of kindness and equity.
If you take a dislike to them,
it may be that you dislike something
and Allah will bring about through it
a great deal of good. (4:19)

Considering the fact that before the advent of Islam the pagan Arabs used to bury their female children alive, make women dance naked in the vicity of the *Ka'ba* during their annual fairs, and treat women as mere chattels and objects of sexual pleasure possessing no rights or position whatsoever, these teachings of the Noble Qur'an were revolutionary.

Unlike other religions, which regarded women as being possessed of inherent sin and wickedness and men as being possessed of inherent virtue and nobility, Islam regards men and women as being of the same essence created from a single soul. The Qur'an declares:

O mankind! Reverence your Guardian-Lord,
who created you from a single person,
created, of like nature, his mate,
and from this pair scattered (like seeds)
countless men and women.
Reverence Allah,
through Whom you demand your mutual (rights),

**and reverence the wombs (that bore you);
for Allah ever watches over you. (4:1)**

The Prophet of Islam (peace be upon him) said, "Women are the twin halves of men."

The Qur'an emphasizes the essential unity of men and women in a most beautiful simile:

**They (your wives) are your garment
and you are a garment for them. (2:187)**

Just as a garment hides our nakedness, so do husband and wife, by entering into the relationship of marriage, secure each other's chastity. The garment gives comfort to the body; so does the husband find comfort in his wife's company and she in his. "The garment is the grace, the beauty, the embellishment of the body, so too are wives to their husbands as their husbands are to them." [1]

Islam does not consider woman "an instrument of the Devil", but rather the Qur'an calls her *muhsana* - a fortress against Satan - because a good woman, by marrying a man, helps him keep to the path of rectitude in his life. It is for this reason that marriage was considered by the Prophet Muhammad (peace be upon him) as a most virtuous act. He said: "When a man marries, he has completed one half of his religion."

He enjoined matrimony on Muslims by saying: "Marriage is part of my way and whoever keeps away from my way is not from me (i.e. is not my follower)."

The Qur'an has given the raison d'etre of marriage in the following words:

**And among His signs is this,
that He has created for you
mates from among yourselves,
that you may dwell in tranquility with them;
and He has put love and mercy between you.
Verily in that are signs for those who reflect. (30:21)**

The Prophet Muhammad (peace be upon him) was full of praise for virtuous and chaste women. He said: "The world and all things in the world are precious but the most precious thing in the world is a virtuous woman."

once told the future khalif, 'Umar: "Shall I not inform you
e best treasure a man can hoard? It is a virtuous wife who
him whenever he looks towards her, and who guards herself
is absent from her."

other occasions the Prophet said: "The best property a man
e is a remembering tongue (about Allah), a grateful heart
elieving wife who helps him in his faith." And again: "The
he whole of it, is a commodity and the best of the commodi-
e world is a virtuous wife."

ore the advent of Islam women were often treated worse
mals. The Prophet wanted to put a stop to all cruelties to
. He preached kindness towards them. He told the Muslims:
Allah in respect of women." And: "The best of you are they
ehave best to their wives." And: "A Muslim must not hate his
and if he be displeased with one bad quality in her, let him be
ed with one that is good." And: "The more civil and kind a
Muslim is to his wife, the more perfect in faith he is."

The Prophet (peace be upon him) was most emphatic in enjoin-
ing upon Muslims to be kind to their women when he delivered his
famous *khutba* on the Mount of Mercy at Arafat in the presence of
one hundred and twenty-four thousand of his Companions who had
gathered there for the *Hajj al-Wada* (Farewell Pilgrimmage). In it he
ordered those present, and through them all those Muslims who were
to come later, to be respectful and kind towards women.

He said: "Fear Allah regarding women. Verily you have married
them with the trust of Allah, and made their bodies lawful with the
word of Allah. You have got (rights) over them, and they have got
(rights) over you in respect of their food and clothing according to
your means."

In Islam a woman is a completely independent personality. She
can make any contract or bequest in her own name. She is entitled
to inherit in her position as mother, as wife, as sister and as daughter. She has perfect liberty to choose her husband.

The pagan society of pre-Islamic Arabia had an irrational preju-
dice against their female children whom they used to bury alive.
The Messenger of Allah (peace be upon him) was totally opposed to
this practice. He showed them that supporting their female children
would act as a screen for them against the fire of Hell.

It is narrated by the Prophet's wife, 'A'isha, that a woman
entered her house with two of her daughters. She asked for charity

but 'A'isha could not find anything except a date, which was given to her. The woman divided it between her two daughters and did not eat any herself. Then she got up and left. When the Prophet (peace be upon him) came to the house, 'A'isha told him about what had happened and he declared that when the woman was brought to account (on the Day of Judgment) about her two daughters they would act as a screen for her from the fires of Hell.

The worst calamity for a woman is when her husband passes away and, as a widow, the responsibility of maintaining the children falls upon her. In the Eastern World, where a woman does not always go out to earn her living, the problems of widowhood are indescribable. The Prophet Muhammad (peace be upon him) upheld the cause of widows. Most of his wives were widows. In an age when widows were rarely permitted to remarry, the Prophet encouraged his followers to marry them. He was always ready to help widows and exhorted his followers to do the same.

Abu Hurairah reported that the Prophet said: "One who makes efforts (to help) the widow or a poor person is like a *mujahid* (warrior) in the path of Allah, or like one who stands up for prayers in the night and fasts in the day."

Woman as mother commands great respect in Islam. The Noble Qur'an speaks of the rights of the mother in a number of verses. It enjoins Muslims to show respect to their mothers and serve them well even if they are still unbelievers. The Prophet states emphatically that the rights of the mother are paramount.

Abu Hurairah reported that a man came to the Messenger of Allah (peace be upon him) and asked: "O Messenger of Allah, who is the person who has the greatest right on me with regards to kindness and attention?" He replied, "Your mother." "Then who?" He replied, "Your mother." "Then who?" He replied, "Your mother." "Then who?" He replied, "Your father."

In another tradition, the Prophet advised a believer not to join the war against the Quraish in defence of Islam, but to look after his mother, saying that his service to his mother would be a cause of his salvation.

Mu'awiyah, the son of Jahimah, reported that Jahimah came to the Prophet (peace be upon him) and said, " Messenger of Allah! I want to join the fighting (in the path of Allah) and I have come to seek your advice." He said, "Then remain in your mother's service because Paradise is under her feet."

The Prophet's followers accepted his teachings and brought about a revolution in their social attitude towards women. They no longer considered women as a mere chattels, but as an integral part of society. For the first time women were given the right to have a share in inheritance. In the new social climate, women rediscovered themselves and became highly active members of society rendering useful service during the wars which the pagan Arabs forced on the emerging Muslim *umma*. They carried provisions for the soldiers, nursed them, and even fought alongside them if it was necessary. It became a common sight to see women helping their husbands in the fields, carrying on trade and business independently, and going out of their homes to satisfy their needs.

'A'isha reported that Saudah bint Zam'ah went out one night. 'Umar saw her and recognised her and said, "By God, O Saudah, why do you not hide yourself from us?" She went back to the Prophet (peace be upon him) and told him about it while he was having supper in her room, and he said, "It is permitted by Allah for you to go out for your needs."

The predominant idea in the teachings of Islam with regard to men and women is that a husband and wife should be fully-fledged partners in making their home a happy and prosperous place, that they should be loyal and faithful to one another, and genuinely interested in each other's welfare and the welfare of their children. A woman is expected to exercise a humanising influence over her husband and to soften the sternness inherent in his nature. A man is enjoined to educate the women in his care so that they cultivate the qualities in which they, by their very nature, excel.

These aspects were much emphasised by the Prophet (peace be upon him). He exhorted men to marry women of piety and women to be faithful to their husbands and kind to their children. He said: "Among my followers the best of men are those who are best to their wives, and the best of women are those who are best to their husbands. To each of such women is set down a reward equivalent to the reward of a thousand martyrs. Among my followers, again, the best of women are those who assist their husbands in their work, and love them dearly for everything, save what is a transgression of Allah's laws."

Once Mu'awiyah asked the Prophet (peace be upon him), "What are the rights that a wife has over her husband?" The Prophet replied, " Feed her when you take your food, give her clothes to wear when you wear clothes, refrain from giving her a slap on the face or abusing her, and do not separate from your wife, except within the house."

Once a woman came to the Prophet with a complaint against her husband. He told her: "There is no woman who removes something to replace it in its proper place, with a view to tidying her husband's house, but that Allah sets it down as a virtue for her. Nor is there a man who walks with his wife hand-in-hand, but that Allah sets it down as a virtue for him; and if he puts his arm round her shoulder in love, his virtue is increased tenfold."

Once he was heard praising the women of the tribe of Quraish, "...because they are the kindest to their children while they are infants and because they keep a careful watch over the belongings of their husbands."

The Shari'ah regards women as the spiritual and intellectual equals of men. The main distinction it makes between them is in the physical realm based on the equitable principle of fair division of labour. It allots the more strenuous work to the man and makes him responsible for the maintenance of the family. It allots the work of managing the home and the upbringing and training of children to the woman, work which has the greatest importance in the task of building a healthy and prosperous society.

It is a fact, however, that sound administration within the domestic field is impossible without a unified policy. For this reason the Shari'ah requires a man, as head of the family, to consult with his family and then to have the final say in decisions concerning it. In doing so he must not abuse his perogative to cause any injury to his wife. Any transgression of this principle involves for him the risk of losing the favour of Allah, because his wife is not his subordinate but she is, to use the words of the Prophet (peace be upon him), 'the queen of her house', and this is the position a true believer is expected to give his wife.

In contrast to these enlightened teachings of Islam in respect of women, Western talk of women's liberation or emancipation is actually a disguised form of exploitation of her body, deprivation of her honour, and degradation of her soul!

2
WOMEN IN SOCIETY

The Family

The family in Islam is a unit in which a man and woman unite to share life together according to the rules and regulations laid down by the Shari'ah. They become as close to each other as a garment is to the body. The husband's honour becomes an integral part of his wife's honour, and vice versa. They share each other's prosperity and adversity. Thus in Islam the bridal couple are united as husband and wife in the presence of witnesses seeking Allah's blessings to increase in mutual love and compassion and agreeing to care for each other in sickness and adversity. This fundamental principle of Islamic marriage, understood and observed by the spouses, is the basis of the institution of Muslim marriage. In the family, the man is charged with the duty of being the leader of the family and the woman is assigned the duty of looking after the household. Even if the man has more responsibility than the woman and thereby has a degree over her, it does not make a husband inherently better than his wife.

The Qur'an contains a verse which says:

> **And in no wise covet those things**
> **in which Allah has bestowed His gifts**
> **more freely on some of you than others:**
> **to men is allotted what they earn,**
> **and to women what they earn... (4:32)**

Commenting on this verse Sheikh Muhammad 'Abduh says that it does not imply that every man is better than every woman or vice versa, but it emphasises that: "each sex, in general, has some preferential advantage over the other, though men have a degree over women."[1]

What is this "degree"? There are different views about it. One view is that it means the qualities of leadership, surveillance and maintenance which are bestowed on men. Another view is that it signifies the tolerance with which men must treat their wives even when in extremely bad moods. Yet another view is that it is man's natural gift from Allah for judging matters pertaining to his family and managing the problems affecting it. However, the consensus of

the scholars is that the "degree" comprises the principle of guardianship and nothing more.

Muhammad 'Abduh feels that guardianship has four elements:
protection surveillance, custody, and maintenance. 'Abd al-'Ati considers that over and above these four elements is the element of obedience. According to 'Abd al-'Ati obedience consists of the following aspects:

1) A wife must neither receive male strangers nor accept gifts from
them without her husband's approval.

2) A husband has the legal right to restrict his wife's freedom of
movement. He may prevent her from leaving her home without his
permission unless there is a necessity or legitimate reason for her to
do otherwise.

However, it is his religious obligation to be compassionate and
not to unreasonably restrict her freedom of movement. If there arises
a conflict between this right of the husband and the rights of the
wife's parents to visit her and be visited by her, the husband's right
prevails in the wider interest of the family. Yet the Shari'ah recommends that he be considerate enough to waive his rights to avoid
shame within the family.

3) A refractory wife has no legal right to object to her husband exercising his disciplinary authority. Islamic law, in common with most
other systems of law, recognises the husband's right to discipline his
wife for disobedience.

4) The wife may not legally object to the husband's right to take
another wife or to exercise his right of divorce. The marital contract
establishes her implicit consent to these rights. However, if she
wishes to restrict his freedom in this regard or to have similar rights,
she is legally allowed to do so. She may stipulate in the marital
agreement that she too will have the right to divorce or that she will
keep the marriage bond only so long as she remains the only wife.
Should he take a second wife, she will have the right to seek a
divorce in accordance with the marriage agreement.[2]

Modesty

Modesty is a virtue which Islam demands of Muslim men and
women. The most powerful verses commanding the believers to be
modest occur in *Surah al-Nur* and begin with the words:

Say to the believing men

> that they should lower their gaze
> and guard their modesty;
> that will make for greater purity for them:
> and Allah is well aware of what they do. (24:31)

The rule of modesty is equally applicable to men and women. A brazen stare by a man at a woman or another man is a breach of correct behaviour. The rule is meant not only to guard women, but is also meant to guard the spiritual good of men.

Looking at the sexual anarchy that prevails in many parts of the world, and which Islam came to check, the need for modesty both in men and women is abundantly clear. However it is on account of the difference between men and women in nature, temperament, and social life, that a greater amount of veiling is required for women than for men, especially in the matter of dress.

A complete code of modesty is laid down in the Qur'an as follows:

> And say to the believing women
> that they should lower their gaze
> and guard their modesty;
> and that they should not display
> their beauty and ornaments
> except what (must ordinarily) appear thereof;
> that they should draw their veils over their bosoms
> and not display their beauty save to their husbands,
> or their fathers or their husbands' fathers,
> or their sons or their husbands' sons,
> or their brothers or their brothers' sons,
> or their sisters' sons, or their women,
> or the slaves whom their right hands possess,
> or male servants free of physical desire,
> or small children who have no sense of sex;
> and that they should not stamp their feet
> in order to draw attention to their hidden ornaments.
> And O believers! Turn all together towards Allah,
> that you may attain bliss. (24:31)

A key term in the above verse is *zinat*. It means both natural beauty and artificial ornaments. The word as used in the above verse seems to include both meanings. Women are asked not to make a display of their figures, not to wear tight clothing that reveals their shapeliness, nor to appear in such dress except to: (1) their husbands, (2) their relatives living in the same house with whom a certain amount of informality is permissible, (3) their women, that is, in the strict sense, their maid-servants who are constantly in attendance on them, but in a more liberal sense, all believing women, (4) old or infirm men-servants, and (5) infants or small children who have not yet got a sense of sex.

While Muslim men are required to cover the body between the navel and the knee, every Muslim woman is asked to cover her whole body excluding the face and hands from all men except her husband. The following traditions of the Prophet (peace be upon him) give us further guidance in the matter:

"It is not lawful for any woman who believes in Allah and the Last Day that she should uncover her hand more than this" - and then he placed his hand on his wrist joint.

"When a woman reaches puberty no part of her body should remain uncovered except her face and the hand up to the wrist joint."

'A'isha reports that once she appeared got up in finery before her nephew, 'Abdullah ibn al-Tufail. The Prophet (peace be upon him) did not approve of it. "I said, 'O Apostle of Allah, he is my nephew.' The Prophet replied, 'When a woman reaches puberty it is not lawful for her to uncover any part of her body except the face and this' - and then he put his hand on the wrist joint as to leave only a little space between the place he gripped and the palm."

Asma', the sister of 'A'isha and daughter of Abu Bakr, came before the Prophet in a thin dress that showed her body. The Prophet turned his eyes away and said, "O Asma'! When a woman reaches puberty, it is not lawful that any part of her body be seen, except this and this" - and then he pointed to his face and the palms of his hands.

Hafsah, daughter of 'Abdur-Rahman, once came before 'A'isha wearing a thin shawl over her head and shoulders. 'A'isha tore it up and put a thick shawl over her.

The Messenger of Allah also said, "Allah has cursed those women who wear clothes yet still remain naked."

The khalif, 'Umar, once said, "Do not clothe your women in clothes that are tight-fitting and reveal the shapeliness of the body."

The above-mentioned traditions make it explicitly clear that the dress of Muslim women must cover the whole body, except for the face and hands, whether in the house or outside, even with her nearest relatives. She must not expose her body to anybody except her husband, and must not wear a dress that shows the curves of her body.

Some scholars, like Muhammad Nasiruddin al-Albani, are of the opinion that, because modern times are particularly full of *fitnah* (mischief), women should go as far as to cover their faces because even the face may attract sexual glances from men.

Shaikh al-Albani says, "We admit that the face is not one of the parts of the body to be covered, but it is not permissible for us to hold to this taking into consideration the corruption of the modern age and the need to stop the means for further corruption."[3]

It is respectfully submitted, however, that in the light of the Prophetic traditions it suffices to cover the body, leaving out the face and hands up to the wrist joints, since this is the specified Islamic covering and it may sometimes be essential for a woman to go about her lawful engagements with her face uncovered. However, if a woman prefers to put on the veil *(burqah)*, she should not be discouraged as this may be a sign of piety and God-consciousness *(taqwah)*.

The rules on dress are slightly relaxed when a woman reaches old age and her sexual attractions have faded. The Qur'an says:

> **Such elderly women**
> **as are past the prospect of marriage,**
> **there is no blame on them**
> **if they lay aside their (outer) garments,**
> **provided they make not**
> **a wanton display of their beauty;**
> **but it is best for them to be modest**
> **and Allah is the One**
> **who sees and knows all things. (24:60)**

However, if a woman is old but still has sexual desires, it is not lawful for her to take off her over-garments. Women at whom people are not possibly going to cast sexual glances but rather look at with respect and veneration are entitled to make use of the relaxation and go about in their houses without wearing an over-garment.

Lowering the Eyes

Islam requires its male and female adherents to avoid illicit sexual relations at all costs. Because the desire to have sexual relationships originates with the look that one person gives another, Islam prohibits a person from casting amorous glances towards another. This is the principle of *ghadd al-basar* (lowering the eyes). Since it is impossible for people to have their eyes fixed constantly to the ground and inconceivable that a man will never see a woman or a woman will never see a man, Islam absolves from blame the first chance look, but prohibits one from casting a second look or continuing to stare at a face which one finds attractive at first sight.

The following traditions of the Prophet (peace be upon him) offer us guidance in this regard:

Jarir says, "I asked the Prophet what I should do if I happened to cast a look (at a woman) by chance. The Prophet replied, 'Turn your eyes away.' "

According to Buraidah, the Prophet told the future fourth khalif, 'Ali, not to cast a second look, for the first look was pardonable but the second was prohibited.

However, there are certain circumstances in which it is permissible for a man to look at another woman. Such circumstances may arise when a woman is obliged to be treated by a male doctor, or has to appear before a judge as a witness, or when a woman is trapped inside a burning house, or is drowning, or when a woman's life or honour is in danger. In such cases, even the prohibited parts of the body of the woman may be seen or touched, and it is not only lawful but obligatory on a man to rescue her from danger, whatever physical contact it may entail.

What is required by Islam in such a situation is that as far as possible the man should keep his intentions pure. But if in spite of that his emotions are a little excited naturally, it is not blameworthy for him to have looked at such a woman, since having contact with her body was not intentional but was necessitated by circumstances, and it is not possible for a man to suppress his natural urges completely.

The Shari'ah also allows a man to look at a woman with the object of reaching a decision about whether he should marry her or not. The following traditions explain the matter further:

Mughirah ibn Shu'bah says, "I sent a message to a woman asking for her hand. The Prophet (peace be upon him) said to me, 'Have a look at her for that will enhance love and mutual regard between you.' "

Abu Hurairah says that he was sitting with the Prophet when a man came and said that he intended to marry a woman from among the *Ansar* (Helpers). The Prophet asked him if he had seen her. He replied in the negative. The Prophet told him to go and have a look at her because the *Ansar* often had a defect in their eyes.

According to Jabir ibn 'Abdullah, the Prophet said that when a man sent a request to a woman for her hand in marriage, he should have a look at her to see if there was anything in her which made him inclined to marry her.

It is thus clear that no man is prohibited from having a look at a woman as such, but that the real idea behind the prohibition is to prevent the evil of illicit intercourse. Therefore what the Prophet has prohibited is only such casting of the eyes as is not essential, as does not serve any social purpose, and as is loaded with sexual motives. This command applies to both Muslim men and Muslim women and is not confined to only one sex.

Maulana Abu'l-A'la Maududi has made a fine psychological distinction, however, between women looking at men and men looking at women. The man, he says, "...is by nature aggressive. If a thing appeals to him, he is urged from within to acquire it. On the other hand, the woman's nature is one of inhibition and escape. Unless her nature is totally corrupted, she can never become so aggressive, bold, and fearless, as to make the first advances towards the male who has attracted her. In view of this distinction, the Legislator (the Prophet) does not regard a woman's looking at other men to be as harmful as a man's looking at other women. In several traditions it has been reported that the Prophet (peace be upon him) let 'A'isha see a performance given by negroes on the occasion of the 'Id. This shows that there is no absolute prohibition on women looking at other men. What is prohibited is for women to sit in the same gathering together with men and stare at them, or look at them in a manner which may lead to evil results.

"The Prophet (peace be upon him) told Fatimah, daughter of Qais, to pass her *'iddah* (waiting term), in the house of Ibn Maktum, the same blind Companion from whom Umm Salamah had been instructed to observe purdah. Qadi Abu Bakr ibn al-'Arabi has related in his *Ahkam al-Qur'an* that Fatimah, daughter of Qais, wanted to pass her waiting term in the house of Umm Sharik. The Prophet did not approve of this for the reason that the house was visited by many people. Therefore he told her to stay in the house of Ibn Maktum who was blind, where she could stay without observing purdah. This shows that the real object of the Prophet was to reduce the chances of any mischief occurring. That is why the lady was not allowed to stay in a house where the chances of possible mischief were greater but allowed to stay in a house where they were less. On the other hand, where there was no such need, women were prohibited from sitting in the same place face to face with other men."[4]

The real object of *ghadd al-basar* (lowering the eyes) is to stop people with evil intentions from casting lewd looks at others. It is common knowlege that a person turns their eyes towards another person innocently in the beginning. If the latter is attractive, the former may go on casting glances and thus drift towards the precipice of sexual attraction and ultimately fornication or adultery. Islam encourages regulated love in order to build up happy family lives since it is healthy families that provide the blocks to construct a healthy society; but it abhors promiscuity which ruins people's family lives and seriously damages people through the ultimate disaster of illicit sexual relationships developing between its adherents. Islam blocks the path that finally leads to active temptation by prohibiting the casting of looks by one person at another except when they do so by chance.

Social Behaviour

The Shari'ah has placed restrictions on men meeting strange women privately. Similarly no man other than her husband is allowed to touch any part of a woman's body. The following traditions of the Prophet (peace be upon him) are worth noting in this connection:

"Beware that you do not call on women who are alone," said the Messenger of Allah. One of the Companions asked, "O Messenger of Allah, what about the younger or the elder brother of the husband?" The Prophet replied, "He is death." (Tirmidhi, Bukhari and Muslim)

"Do not call on women in the absence of their husbands, because Satan might be circulating in any of you like blood." (Tirmidhi)

According to 'Amr ibn al-'As, the Prophet forbade men to call on women without the permission of their husbands. (Tirmidhi)

"From this day no man is allowed to call on a woman in the absence of her husband unless he is accompanied by one or two other men." (Tirmidhi)

The Prophet said, "The one who touches the hand of a woman without having a lawful relationship with her, will have an ember placed on his palm on the Day of Judgement." (Takmalah, Fath al-Qadir)

'A'ishah says that the Prophet accepted the oath of allegiance from women only verbally, without taking their hands into his own hand. He never touched the hand of a woman who was not married to him. (Bukhari)

Umaimah, daughter of Ruqaiqah, said that she went to the Prophet in the company of some other women to take the oath of allegiance. He made them promise that they would abstain from idolatry, stealing, adultery, slander, and disobedience to the Prophet. When they had taken the oath, they requested that he take their hands as a mark of allegiance. The Prophet said, "I do not take the hands of women. Verbal affirmation is enough." (Nasa'i and Ibn Majah)

According to Maulana Maududi these commandments apply in respect of young women. He says, "It is lawful to sit with women of advanced age in privacy and touching them is also not prohibited. It has been reported that Sayyiduna Abu Bakr used to visit the clan where he had been suckled and shook hands with the old women. It has been reported that Sayyiduna 'Abdullah ibn Zubair used to have his feet and head pressed gently for relief by an old woman. This distinction between old and young women itself shows that the real object is to prevent such mixing of the sexes as may lead to evil results."[5]

It is most unfortunate, however, that in spite of this guidance from the Prophet (peace be upon him) many Muslims have adopted the Western system of shaking hands with women, using these traditions in respect of old women as a justification. This is clearly an unreasonable extension of the permission. It is, therefore, submitted that the Muslims the world over, and 'ulama in particular, must pause to reflect and stop this un-Islamic practice which has crept into our society. There cannot be a better form of greeting than uttering 'as-salamu 'alaikum '(peace be upon you) and greeting back with *'wa alaikum as-salam* '(and peace be upon you too).

The Shari'ah wants people to live in their houses in peace and privacy. It therefore commands a Muslim, when visiting friends, relatives or strangers not to enter their houses without seeking their permission. The Qur'an particularly forbids him to enter their houses without alerting the women of the house so that he does not surprise them in a condition in which he would not normally see them.

However, children do not have to seek such permission until they reach the age of puberty and sexual awareness stirs in them:

> **When your children attain puberty,**
> **they should ask for leave before entering the house,**
> **just as their elders asked it before them... (24:58)**

The Holy Qur'an also gives categories of people who should not enter anybody else's house without permission:

> **O believers! Do not enter houses**
> **other than your own**
> **until you have taken permission;**
> **and when you enter a house,**
> **greet the people therein with salutation. (33:33)**

At the beginning of Islam, the Arabs could not grasp the real significance of these commands. Therefore they used to peep into houses from the outside.[6] Once when the Prophet (peace be upon him) was in his room, a person peeped through the lattice. The Prophet said:

"If I had known that you were peeping, I would have poked something into your eye. The command to ask permission has been given to safeguard people against the evil look." (Bukhari)

Then the Prophet publicly announced: "If a person peeps into somebody else's house without permission the people of the house will be justified if they injure his eye." (Muslim)

No matter how urgent the need is, no-one is allowed to enter anyone else's house without permission. The Qur'an says:

> **...and when you ask women for an article,**
> **ask for it from behind a curtain;**
> **this is a purer way**

for your hearts and theirs. (33:53)

These restrictions also apply to household servants. Once Bilal or Anas asked Fatimah, the daughter of the Prophet, to hand him her child. She handed it to him by stretching her hand from behind a curtain. It is noteworthy that both these men were the personal attendants of the Prophet (peace be upon him) and he used to affectionately address them as *"Ya Bunayya"* (O my son).

The real purpose behind those restrictions is to safeguard men and women against evil inclinations. By keeping a safe distance between them, the Shari'ah ensures that they do not grow too familar and free with one another which may make them drift towards sexual intimacy.

Beautification and Adornment

The Qur'an lays down the code of conduct for women in the following words:

> **And play your role by being in your houses**
> **and do not keep exhibiting**
> **your beauty and decorations**
> **like what used to happen**
> **in the *Jahiliyyah* period (before Islam). (33:33)**

Abu Bakr al-Jassas says in explaining this verse, "This verse points out the fact that women are ordered to play their role in the house and are forbidden from loitering outside of their houses."[7]

It was revealed when the Muslim *ummah* was being formed in Madina as an example for the coming generations of Muslims. It sought to put an end to the *Jahiliyyah* practices of the pagan Arabs. The khalif 'Umar remarked: "By Allah, we did not give any position to women in the *Jahiliyyah* period until such time that Allah sent His command in respect of them and apportioned for them the role that was to be theirs." (Muslim)

Under this apportionment women were given the role of making their own homes the centres of their attention rather than going about exhibiting their physical charms and worldly possessions. The Prophet (peace be upon him) said that the following type of women constitute one of the categories of the dwellers of Hell:

"Those women who seem naked even when dressed and those

who walk flirtingly and those who plait their heads like the humps
of camels, thus inviting people's attention, will not enter Paradise
nor will they smell its fragrance even though its fragrance can be
smelt from a very long distance." (Muslim)

Islam, however, does not prohibit beautification *(zinat)* on the
part of women as long as it is not done in a way that injuriously
interferes with the limbs or the body.

In ancient times there were many kinds of defacement practised
on the bodies of men and animals, partly on account of superstition
or pagan custom and partly on account of the craze for fashion and
display. Examples of this were tattooing, sharpening or spacing the
teeth, shaving or plucking the hair, wearing hair pieces, etc. Many
of these practices still survive and are, in fact, getting more and
more refined.

Since all these practices change or seriously interfere with the
natural creation of Allah, the Prophet (peace be upon him) cursed
those who indulged in them for the purpose of mere beautification.
One report says,

"The Messenger of Allah cursed women who tattooed, and
those who got themseves tattooed, those who engaged in sharpening
the teeth (as a mark of beauty) and those who had their teeth sharp-
ened." (Bukhari and Muslim)

The Messenger of Allah cursed women who had spaces made
between their teeth in order to increase their beauty, thus changing
the creation of Allah.

A third report says, "The Messenger of Allah cursed the women
who plucked hair and those who were employed to pluck the eyebrows." (Abu Dawud)

This method of beautification would include the modern practice of shaving the eyebrows and then painting on new ones, or
shaving certain hair and leaving the eyebrows to look like two
inverted crescents.

However, if a woman has some obtrusive hairs on her face
which are a problem and embarrassment for her, she may remove
them. When 'A'ishah was approached by the young wife of Abu
Is'haq who wished to remove her facial hairs in order to look beautiful for her husband, she advised her to do so. (Reported by at-
Tabarani) On this basis some Hanafi jurists are of the opinion that
there in no harm in removing the hairs from a woman's face and
applying cosmetics if it is done with the permission of the husband,

in order to please him and with a good intention. But Imam al-Nawawi opposes even removing the hairs on a woman's face because he considers the practice similar to plucking hair.

A fourth report says: "'A'ishah reported that the Messenger of Allah (peace be upon him) cursed women who wore hair pieces and the women who aided in this practice." (Bukhari)

This method of beautification would include the modern practice of wearing wigs. It consists of using a plait of one woman's hair or artificial hair and joining it to another woman's hair with the object of making the woman's hair appear very long and beautiful.

Mu'awiyah, while holding a plait of such hair in his hands during his address to the Muslims, castigated the *'ulama:* "Where are your learned men gone? (meaning why did they not stop women from using such hair) I heard the Messenger of Allah stop them from using this." He also said, "Undoubtedly the Israelites destroyed themselves when their women adopted such things." (Bukhari)

The Shari'ah also requires women to abstain from displaying their "decorations" except to a restricted circle of people. The Qur'an says:

> And say to the believing women
> that they should lower their gaze
> and guard their modesty;
> and that they should not display
> their beauty and ornaments
> except what (must ordinarily) appear thereof;
> that they should draw their veils over their bosoms and
> not display their beauty save to their husbands,
> or their fathers, or their husbands' fathers,
> or their sons, or their husbands' sons,
> or their brothers or their brothers' sons,
> or their sisters' sons, or their women,
> or the slaves whom their right hands possess,
> or male servants free of physical desire,
> or small children who have no sense of sex;
> and that they should not stamp their feet in order to
> draw attention to their hidden ornaments.
> And O believers! Turn all together towards Allah,
> that you may attain bliss. (24:31)

Thus, the following people fall in the exceptional category to whom decorations can be displayed by a woman:

1) Her husband.
2) Her father, including maternal and paternal grandfathers.
3) Her husband's father. He is also like her own father.
4) Her son, including grandsons from her son's side or her daughter's side.
5) Her husband's son by another woman, provided that he is staying with her, and she is looking after him as her son.
6) Her brother, whether full, consanguine, or uterine (that is to say, real or step).
7) Her brother's son.
8) Her sister's son.
9) Muslim women and other women of good character.
10) Her female slaves or servants. However, some *'ulama* even include male slaves or servants in the excepted category.
11) Men who have no sexual desire (e.g. eunuchs).
12) Children who have not yet developed sexual feelings.
13) Her uncle, whether paternal or maternal.

It is noteworthy that the above verse of the Noble Qur'an does not mention uncle, but uncle is included in the exceptional category on the basis of a tradition of the Prophet (peace be upon him). The Prophet said, "The uncle (maternal or paternal) is of the same degree as one's father." (Muslim)

Let us here give a little more consideration to the women to whom another woman is permitted to display her finery. These are the women with whom she has blood or family relations. It should be borne in mind that the foregoing Qur'anic verse implies only women of good character. Other women who may not be well known to her or who are notorious for their evil ways or who may be of doubtful character are excluded from this permission, because contact with them might easily lead to disastrous results. That is why the *khalif* 'Umar wrote to Abu 'Ubaidah ibn al-Jarrah, the Governor of Syria, to prohibit the Muslim women from going to the baths with the women of the *Ahl al-Kitab* (the People of the Book). (At-Tabari, Ibn Jazir) According to Ibn 'Abbas too: "...a Muslim woman is not allowed to display herself before the women of the unbelievers and non-Muslim poll-tax payers *(Ahl al-Dhimmah)* any more than she can display herself before other men." (At-Tabari)

This distinction between women on grounds of character and

religion is intended to safeguard Muslim women against the influence of women whose moral and cultural background is either not known or is objectionable from the Islamic point of view. However, the Shari'ah allows Muslim women to mix freely with non-Muslim women who are of good character. It is important to note that permission to display *zinat* does not include permission to display those parts of the body which fall within the female *satr*. Thus *zinat* covers decorations, ornaments, clothing, hair-dos, etc. that women are by nature fond of showing in their houses. But tight jeans, short blouses, sleeveless dresses are not counted as *zinat* for they also reveal that *satr*.

The Shari'ah further requires a woman not to stamp on the ground while walking, lest her hidden decorations should be revealed by their jingle, and thus attract the attention of passers-by.

Writing about these restrictions, Maulana Maududi says: "It cannot, however, be claimed that a display of fineries will turn every woman into a prostitute, nor that every man who sees her will become an adulterer. But, at the same time, nobody can deny that if women go about in full make-up and mix freely with men, it is likely to result in countless open and secret, moral and material disadvantages for society." [8]

As against this view, the Egyptian scholars, notably 'Abbas Mahmud al-'Aqqad, are of the view that these restrictions were only imposed on the wives of the Prophet (peace be upon him) and other Muslim women are not bound by them. 'Aqqad says, "We should discuss this point in the light of the fact that the command to stay at home was merely addressed to the wives of the Prophet (peace be upon him) with particular reference to them without referring it to Muslim women in general. It is for this reason that the verse begins with the statement of Allah:

O women of the Prophet,
you are not like other women. (33:32)[9]

It is respectfully submitted that this view of Al-'Aqqad needs reconsideration. There are a number of verses in the Qur'an which, though apparently laying down "dos" and "don'ts" for our Prophet and for the other Prophets (peace be upon all of them) preceding him, contain clear messages for Muslims in general, nay for all mankind. And Al-'Aqqad contradicts himself when he quotes the following verse of the Holy Qur'an:

O you who believe! Do not enter the Prophet's house until leave
is given you for a meal,
(and then) not (so early as) to wait for its preparation;
but when you are invited, enter;
and when you have taken your meal, disperse,
without seeking familar talk.
Such (behaviour) annoys the Prophet.
He is ashamed to dismiss you,
but Allah is not ashamed (to tell you) the truth.
And when you ask his womenfolk for anything you want,
ask them from behind a screen;
that makes for greater purity
for your hearts and for theirs.
Nor is it right for you
that you should annoy Allah's Apostle, or that you should marry
his widows after him at any time.
Truly such a thing is an enormity in Allah's sight. (33:53)

This verse apparently lays down a code of manners for the
believers when entering the house of the Prophet (peace be upon
him) and taking food there.

After quoting this verse, Al-'Aqqad says: "And this is part of
the etiquette of visiting people with which all visitors should be
well disciplined."[10] In other words, he agrees that this *ayat*, which is
specific to the house of the Prophet (peace be upon him) and taking
food there, in reality contains rules applicable to all believers who
want to enter somebody else's house. If from this special case a rule
of general application can be deduced by Al-'Aqqad, there seems no
reason why he should refuse to deduce a rule of general application
for Muslim women from the verse addressed to the wives of the
Prophet. Moreover, this view seems to get support from a tradition
of the Prophet in which he said: "...a woman who freely mixes with
other people and shows off her decorations is without light and
virtue." (At-Tirmidhi)

Hence we may conclude that no Muslim woman should display
her *zinat* (decoration) before others intentionally, but she is not held
responsible for something which cannot be helped e.g. her stature,
physical build, gait, etc. nor for uncovering her hand or face when

there is a genuine need to do so and without any intention of attracting men. In such cases it is the responsibility of Muslim men not to cast evil glances at women with the intention of drawing pleasure from them. The Qur'an ordains:

Say to believing men to lower their eyes. (24:30)

Guests

Very often, a man may receive male visitors and guests in his house. In such a situation the question may arise whether the wife of the host can come forward to serve food and drink to them. If a woman's husband is not present when his guests arrive, she should not serve them. However, if her husband is present and the guests are known friends, relatives and well-wishers, a woman may come forward to serve them with food and drink provided that she is properly dressed and her manners, movements and method of talking are such that they are not likely to encourage evil in them or arouse their passions and thereby become a source of *fitnah* (mischief).

We have a very good example in the following: "When 'Abdur-Rashid al-Sa'adi got married, he invited the Prophet (peace be upon him) and his Companions. His wife, Umm Asyad, prepared the food alone and served it herself. She soaked some dates in a stone bowl overnight. When the Prophet finished eating, she offered him the water, after stirring it well, as a present." (At-Tirmidhi and Abu Dawud)

If a woman is not properly dressed, it is better that she does not come forward to serve guests. In this case she should pass out the food and drinks to her husband and he should entertain the guests and visitors on his own.

Public Baths and Swimming Pools

A Muslim woman should not use public baths *(hammam)* or swimming pools because these places are likely to be a cause of her exposing herself to evil influences. The following tradition treats this point: "Some womens from Homs or from Sham (now the area of Damascus) came to 'A'ishah. She asked, 'Do you enter the public baths? I heard the Messenger of Allah saying that a woman who undresses anywhere else other than in her own house tears off the *satr* which lies between her and her Lord .' " (At-Tirmidhi and Abu Dawud)

If the public baths and swimming pools are mixed, with both men and women using them, it is all the more objectionable. At one stage the Prophet (peace be upon him) forbade both men and women to enter public ɔath-houses but later he allowed men to use them on the condition that they were never naked. "The Messenger of Allah, may Allah bless him and grant him peace, forbade all men to enter public baths but later allowed them to enter them wearing waist-wrappers."

If a wealthy man builds a private pool on his own property there is no harm in him and his wife using it together. However, if he has more than one wife, he should not bathe with more than one at a time, and, if he has grown-up sons, they should not bathe together with their mothers or step-mothers.

Dance-Halls and Gymnasiums

Places in which men and women dance together are totally at odds with the ethos of Muslim society and the Shari'ah does not tolerate the participation of Muslim men and women in this activity because it may so easily prove the first step towards greater evils such as adultery and fornication. Dancing is most certainly not compatible with the simple, purposeful lives that all Muslims should lead.

Mixed gymnasiums where women remove their clothes and wear skin-tight costumes for doing physical exercises are also against the dictates of the Shari'ah.

The Mosque

The Prophet of Allah (peace be upon him) granted permission to Muslim women to attend the mosque and pray standing behind the rows of men. He even advised the Companions:

"Do not prevent the female servants of Allah from going to the mosque."

And husbands were specifically told by him:

"When your womenfolk ask you for permission to attend the mosque, do not prevent them."

Of course this permission to attend the mosques was on the condition that women strictly observed the various restrictions imposed upon them by the Shari'ah regarding dress, etc., and it is known that the Prophet (peace be upon him) considered it preferable for women to pray in their own homes rather than attend the mosques. This is borne out by the following incident.

Once the wife of Abu Hamid Sa'adi pleaded with the Prophet to be allowed to attend his mosque (the Prophet's Mosque in Madina) as she was very fond of offering prayers behind him. He told her, "What you say is right, but it is better for you to offer prayer in a closed room than in a courtyard. Your prayer in a courtyard is better than on a verandah, and your offering prayer in the mosque of your own locality is better than your coming to our mosque for it." Thereafter she appointed a room for offering prayers and continued offering prayers there till her death, never even once going to the mosque.

There is a clear tradition of the Prophet (peace be upon him) encouraging women to offer their prayers inside their houses: "The best mosques for women are the inner parts of their houses."

Since the Prophet had not forbidden women to attend the mosques, they continued to come to the mosques. But after his death it became increasingly clear that it was not in keeping with the dignity and honour of Muslim women to come to the mosques for prayers, especially at night, because men, being what they were, would tease them. Thereforethe Khalif 'Umar told women not to come to the mosques, but to offer their prayers inside their own houses. The women of Madina resented this prohibition and complained to 'A'isha. But they received a fitting reply from her: "If the Prophet knew what 'Umar knows, he would not have granted you permission to go out (to the mosque)."

'A'isha also prevented women from going to the mosques. When she was told that the Prophet (peace be upon him) had permitted them to attend the mosques, she replied: "Had the customs and manners which women have adopted since the Prophet's death been there in his lifetime, he too would have prevented them."

Now, what 'A'isha said by way of admonition was in the context of what happened immediately after the death of the Prophet. But what is happening today 1350 years after his death is much more serious in the context of modern fashions and manners. It would probably have shocked 'A'isha beyond measure and she would have reinforced her admonition. Be that as it may, the fact remains that our Prophet did grant permission to women to attend the mosques.

In the modern world a new situation has arisen. There are many Muslims living in Western countries, and Western culture and fash-

ions have affected women, even in the East. In addition, the economic tyranny of today has forced many women to work in factories and offices to earn their living. These developments have largely contributed to making many Muslims neglectful of their prayers.
We Muslims have to find ways and means of encouraging Muslim
women to be particular about their prayers. With due respect to what
the khalif, 'Umar, and the Mother of the Believers, 'A'isha, said, it
appears to this humble writer that such a way can be found by
reverting to the original Prophetic tradition, that is to say, permitting
Muslim women to attend the mosques to offer their prayers, subject
to all the restrictions laid down by the Prophet (peace be upon him)
about their dress etc.

People generally learn by example. Therefore the chances are
that, if women started coming to the mosque for prayer, a social
pressure would start building up that would make Muslim women
feel the urge to come to the mosque to offer their prayers and give
up their neglectful attitude. However, it goes without saying that
proper arrangements would have to be made for Muslim women to
attend the mosques. They must not be allowed to mingle with the
men, and their rows must be kept separate from those of the men,
preferably behind them, because this is what was approved by the
Prophet (peace be upon him).

It is reported by Abu Hurairah that the Prophet (peace be upon
him) said: "The best row for men is the first, and the worst for them
is the last. The best row for women is the last, and the worst is the
first." (Muslim)

It is well known that, in the time of the Prophet, women were
permitted to attend the mosques subject to the condition that they
satisfied the various restrictions imposed on them by the Shari'ah,
such as the putting on of a *jalbab* (a large sheet used for covering
the entire body), wearing simple and dignified clothes, not using
any perfume, avoiding ostentatious display of ornament, etc. Therefore, if the suggestion of this writer is accepted, efforts will have to
be made to persuade Muslim women who want to attend the
mosques to start complying with the traditional restrictions on dress,
etc. But what has been suggested above should in no way be taken
to mean that all women should be required to attend the mosque and
indeed those who feel that their houses are as good as the mosque
should be encouraged to offer their prayers there.

3

MARRIAGE AND SEXUAL RELATIONS

Allah has created men and women as company for one another, and so that they can procreate and live in peace and tranquility according to the commandments of Allah and the directions of His Messenger. The Qur'an says:

> And among His signs is this,
> that He created for you mates
> from among yourselves,
> that you may dwell in tranquility with them,
> and He has put love and mercy
> between your hearts.
> Undoubtedly in these are signs
> for those who reflect. (30:21)

> And Allah has made for you
> your mates of your own nature,
> and made for you, out of them,
> sons and daughters and grandchildren,
> and provided for you
> sustenance of the best. (16:72)

These verses of the Noble Qur'an clearly show that in contrast to other religions like Christianity, Buddhism, Jainism etc. which consider celibacy or monasticism as a great virtue and a means of salvation, Islam considers marriage as one of the most virtuous and approved institutions.

The Messenger of Allah (peace be upon him) declared, "There is no monasticism in Islam." He further ordained, "O you young men! Whoever is able to marry should marry, for that will help him to lower his gaze and guard his modesty." (Al-Bukhari)

Modesty was regarded as a great virtue by the Prophet. He said, "Modesty is part of faith." (Al-Bukhari)

The importance of the institution of marriage receives its greatest emphasis from the following *hadith* of the Prophet, "Marriage is my *sunna*. Whosoever keeps away from it is not from me."

With these Qur'anic injunctions and the guidance from the Prophet (peace be upon him) in mind, we shall examine the institution of marriage in the Shari'ah.

The word *zawaj* is used in the Qur'an to signify a pair or a mate.[1] But in common parlance it stands for marriage. Since the family is the nucleus of Islamic society, and marriage is the only way to bring families into existence, the Prophet (peace be upon him) insisted upon his followers entering into marriage.

The Shari'ah prescribes rules to regulate the functioning of the family so that both spouses can live together in love, security, and tranquility. Marriage in Islam has aspects of both *'ibadah* (worship) of Allah and *mu'amalah* (transactions between human beings). In its *'ibadah* aspect, marriage is an act pleasing to Allah because it is in accordance with his commandments that husband and wife love each other and help each other to make efforts to continue the human race and rear and nurse their children to become true servants of Allah.

In its *mu'amalah* aspect, marriage being a lawful response to the basic biological instinct to have sexual intercourse and to procreate children, the Shari'ah has prescribed detailed rules for translating this response into a living human institution reinforced by a whole framework of legally enforceable rights and duties, not only of the spouses, but also of their offspring.

These aspects are beautifully explained in a tradition of the Prophet. It is narrated by Anas that the Messenger of Allah (peace be upon him) said, "When a man marries, he has fulfilled half of his religion, so let him fear Allah regarding the remaining half."

The Prophet considered marriage for a Muslim as half of his religion because it shields him from promiscuity, adultery, fornication, homosexuality etc, which ultimately lead to many other evils like slander, quarrelling, homicide, loss of property and disintegration of the family.

According to the Prophet (peace be upon him) the remaining half of the faith can be saved by *taqwa*.

Conditions of Marriage

Careful consideration of the Qur'anic injunctions and the traditions of the Prophet (peace be upon him) clearly show that marriage is compulsory *(wajib)* for a man who has the means to easily pay the *mahr* (dowry) and to support a wife and children, and is healthy, and fears that if does not marry, he may be tempted to commit fornication *(zina)*. It is also compulsory for a woman who has no other means of maintaining herself and who fears that her sexual urge may push her into fornication. But even for a person who has a strong will to control his sexual desire, who has no wish to have children, and who feels that marriage will keep him away from his devotion to Allah, it is commendable *(mandub)* [2]

However, according to the Maliki school, under certain conditions it is obligatory *(fard)* for a Muslim to marry even if he is not in a position to earn his living:

(i) If he fears that by not marrying he will commit fornication *(zina)*.

(ii) If he is unable to fast to control his passions or his fasting does not help him to refrain from *zina*.

(iii) Even if he is unable to find a slave girl or a destitute girl to marry.[3]

However some jurists suggest that if a man cannot procure a lawful livelihood, he must not marry because if he marries without any hope of getting lawful bread, he may commit theft, and in order to avoid one evil (his passions) he may become the victim of another (theft).[4]

The Hanafi school considers marriage as obligatory *(fard)* for a man:

(i) If he is sure that he will commit *zina* if he does not marry.

(ii) If he cannot fast to control his passions or even if he can fast, his fast does not help him to control his passion.

(iii) If he cannot get a slave-girl to marry.

(iv) If he is able to pay the dowry *(mahr)* and to earn a lawful livelihood.

Marriage is forbidden *(haram)* to a man, according to the Hanafi school, if he does not possess the means to maintain his wife and children or if he suffers from an illness, serious enough to affect his wife and progeny.

It is not desirable *(makruh)* for a man who possesses no sexual desire at all or who has no love for children or who is sure to be slackened in his religious obligations as a result of marriage.[5]

In a beautiful tradition the Prophet (peace be upon him) has given the most important point that should weigh with every

Muslim in selecting his bride: "Whoever marries a woman solely
for her power and position, Allah will only increase him in humiliation. Whoever marries a woman solely for her wealth, Allah will
only increase him in poverty. Whoever marries a woman because of
her beauty, Allah will only increase him in ugliness. But whoever
marries a woman in order that he may restrain his eyes, observe cau-
tiousness, and treat his relations kindly, Allah puts a blessing in her
for him and in him for her."

In order that problems should not arise after marriage the
Prophet (peace be upon him) recommended that, in the selection of
his bride, a man should see her before betrothal lest blindness of
choice or an error of judgment should defeat the very purpose of
marriage. But this "seeing" is not to be taken as a substitute for the
"courtship" of the West. The man should not gaze passionately at
his bride-to-be, but only have a critical look at her face and hands to
acquaint himself with her personality and beauty.[6]

However, if a man so desires, he may appoint a woman to go
and interview the proposed bride, so that she may fully describe the
type of girl she is.[7]

Since believing men and women are referred to in the Qur'an, a
woman also has the right to look at her potential husband.[8]

The special permission for men and women to see each other
with a view to matrimony does not contravene the code of conduct
for believing men and women to lower their gaze and be modest
which is laid down in the Holy Qur'an.

Ijbar: a Safety Valve

The consent of both the man and the women is an essential element of marriage, and the Qur'an gives women a substantial role in
choosing their own life partners. It lays down:

> **Do not prevent them**
> **from marrying their husbands**
> **when they agree between themselves**
> **in a lawful manner. (2: 232)**

However, Imam Malik, one of the four great Imams of the
Sunni schools of Islamic jurisprudence, gives a slightly restrictive
interpretation to this verse and makes the choice of partner by a
Muslim girl subject to the over-ruling power or *ijbar* of her father

or guardian in the interests of the girl herself.

It may sometimes happen that in her immaturity or over-zealousness, a girl may want to marry a man about whom she has distorted information or who does not possess good character or who lacks proper means of livelihood. In such a case, it is better, or rather incumbent upon the girl's father or guardian, that, in the wider interests of the girl, he restrains her from marrying such a worthless man and finds a suitable person to be her husband. Generally speaking, such marriages arranged by fathers and guardians work better than a marriage brought about through western courtship.

The case of Abu Juham bin Hudhaifah and Mu'awiyah ibn Abu Sufyan is relevant here. They proposed marriage to Fatimah bint Ghaith. The Prophet (peace be upon him) advised Fatimah not to marry either of them on the grounds that Mu'awiyah was then a pauper and Abu Juham was cruel and harsh. So she married Usamah.

The Free Consent of the Parties

The Qur'an (4:21) refers to marriage as a *mithaq*, i.e. a solemn covenant or agreement between husband and wife, and enjoins that it be put down in writing. Since no agreement can be reached between the parties unless they give their consent to it, marriage can be contracted only with the free consent of the two parties. The Prophet (peace be upon him) said, "The widow and the divorced woman shall not be married until their order is obtained, and the virgin shall not be married until her consent is obtained." (Al-Bukhari)

This aspect is greatly emphasised by Imam Bukhari. He, in fact, gave one of the chapters in his *Sahih* the significant title: "When a man gives his daughter in marriage and she dislikes it, the marriage shall be annulled."

Once a virgin girl came to the Prophet (peace be upon him) and said that her father had married her to a man against her wishes. The Prophet gave her the right to repudiate the marriage. (Abu Dawud)

Divorced women are also given freedom to contract a second marriage. The Holy Qur'an says,

And when you divorce women,

and they have come to the end
of their waiting period,
hinder them not from marrying other men
if they have agreed with each other
in a fair manner. (2: 232)

With regard to widows, the Qur'an says,

And if any of you die
and leave behind wives,
they bequeath thereby to their widows
(the right to) one year's maintenance
without their being obliged
to leave (their husband's home),
but if they leave (the residence)
of their own accord,
there is no blame on you
for what they do with themselves
in a lawful manner. (2:234)

Thus widows are also at liberty to re-marry, even within the period mentioned above; and if they do so they must forgo their claim to traditional maintenance during the remainder of the year. However, it must be remembered that the power of *ijbar* given to the father or the guardian by the Maliki school over their selection of life-partner obtains in all the situations considered above, namely, whether the daughter or the ward is a virgin or divorcee or widow.

Prohibited Marriage Partners
Under the Shari'ah, marriages between men and women standing in a certain relationship to one another are prohibited. These prohibited degrees are either of a permanent nature or a temporary nature.

The permanently prohibited degrees of marriage are laid down in the Holy Qur'an:

And marry not those women
whom your fathers married,
except what has already happened

(of that nature) in the past.
Lo! it was ever lewdness
and abomination, and an evil way.
Forbidden unto you
are your mothers and your daughters,
and your sisters and your father's sisters
and your mother's sisters,
and your brother's daughters
and your sister's daughters,
and your foster-mothers and your foster-sisters,
and your mothers-in-law and your step-daughters
who are under your mother-in-law
and your step-daughters who are under your protection
(born) of your women unto whom you have gone into
-- but if you have not gone into them,
then it is no sin for you (to marry their daughters) --
and the wives of your sons from your own loins,
and that you should have two sisters together,
except what has already happened
(of that nature) in the past.
Allah is ever-Forgiving, Merciful. (4:22 - 24)

From the above verses, it is clear that a Muslim must never marry the following:
1) His mother
2) His step-mother (this practice continues in Yoruba land in Nigeria, where in some cases the eldest son inherits the youngest wife of his father)
   3) His grandmother (including father's and mother's mothers and all preceding mothers eg. great grandmothers)
4) His daughter (including granddaughters and beyond)
5) His sister (whether full, consanguine or uterine)
6) His father's sisters (including paternal grandfather's sisters)
7) His mother's sisters (including maternal grandmother's sisters)
8) His brother's daughters
9) His foster mother
10) His foster mother's sister
11) His sister's daughter
12) His foster sister
13) His wife's mother

14) His step-daughter (i.e. a daughter by a former husband of a woman he has married if the marriage has been consummated. However, if such a marriage was not consummated, there is no prohibition)
15) His real son's wife
A great wisdom lies behind these prohibitions on the grounds of consanguinity, affinity, and fosterage. No social cohesion can exist if people do not keep these prohibitions in their minds while contracting marriages.

Temporary prohibitions are those which arise only on account of certain special circumstances in which the parties are placed. If the circumstances change, the prohibition also disappears. They are as follows:
1) A man must not have two sisters as wives at the same time nor can he marry a girl and her aunt at the same time.
2) A man must not marry a woman who is already married. However this impediment is removed immediately the marriage is dissolved either by the death of her former husband, or by divorce, followed by completion of the period of *'iddah* (retreat).
3) A man must not have more than four wives at one time. This impediment is, of course, removed as soon as one of the wives dies or is divorced.
4) A man must not marry a woman during her *'iddah*.
Regarding this last prohibition, the Qur'an expects Muslims to act with the utmost propriety and righteousness. It lays down:

...but do not make a secret contract with them
except in honourable terms,
nor resolve on the tie of marriage
till the term prescribed is fulfilled. (2:235)

This means that a man must not make a specific proposal of marriage to a woman during the time of her *'iddah* after the death of her husband or an irrevocable divorce. However, he can send a message saying, for instance, "I wish to find a woman of good character". But if a woman is in the *'iddah* of a divorce which is revocable where *raja'*(return) is possible, a man must not send her even an implied invitation to marry him, because she is still considered as the lawful wife of the first husband. In fact, this restriction is most beneficial because it prevents a man from becoming an instrument of breaking up a family where there are still chances of reconciliation between the wife and husband even though they are moving away from each other.

Two Suitors Seeking to Marry the Same Girl

The Prophet (peace be upon him) disapproved of two persons competing with one another to secure marriage with the same girl. This is because such a situation is likely to develop bitter enmity between two Muslim brothers.

The Prophet said, "A believer is a brother of a believer. Hence it is not lawful for him to bargain upon the bargain of a brother, nor propose for (the hand of a girl) after the marriage proposal of his brother, until the latter (voluntarily) withdraws the proposal."

Imam Abu Hanifa, Imam Shafi'i, and Imam Malik, all hold the view that it is a sin to put a proposal of marriage against the proposal of another Muslim brother. However, if a marriage is contracted in this wrongful way it will be sufficient if the second suitor who was successful seeks the forgiveness of the first suitor and of Allah.[9] But Imam Dhahiri considers such a marriage void. It is respectfully submitted that the former view is more rational and sound.

Relative Positions of Men and Women in Marriage

Islam builds a strong society by making individual families well-knit and strong. It is with this end in view that Islam assigns specific roles to men and women so that they may work in peace and harmony to make happy and healthy families. Islam does not leave men and women to dissipate their energies on needless speculation or squabbles about talk of "equality", but prescribes the channels in which men and women must move if they are to live smooth, good lives. The Qur'an says:

> **Men are the protectors and maintainers of women,**
> **because Allah has given the one**
> **more (strength) than the other,**
> **and because they support them from their means.**
> **Therefore righteous women are devotedly obedient**
> **and guard in (the husband's) absence**
> **what Allah would would have them guard.**

**As to those women on whose part
you fear disloyalty and ill-conduct,
admonish them (first),
(next) refuse to share their beds,
and (last) beat them (lightly);
but if they return to obedience,
seek not against them means of annoyance. (4:34)**

This verse declares men to be the *qawwamun,* i.e. protectors and maintainers in relation to women in order to keep the family peaceful and united. The word *qawwamun* signifies a person who takes the responsibility of safe-guarding the interests of another person.

By reason of their greater physical strength and capacity for strenuous work, men are, generally speaking, better qualified to act as *qawwamun* in relation to women. Moreover, it is necessary for the smooth functioning of a family that there should be a head who possesses the capacity to settle things among the members of the family and, if necessary, give orders to them and ensure their compliance. It is for this reason that the wife is asked to obey her husband and children are asked to obey their parents.

However, it should be borne in mind that the wife is not bound to obey her husband if what he asks her to do is against Allah's injunctions, because obedience to Allah comes first.

The foregoing verse prescribes certain measures which should be taken in settling disputes which might arise between married couples:

1) Admonition

As a first step, the husband should admonish his wife in a polite manner. If this proves effective, there is no need to resort to a stronger measure.

2) Suspension of Conjugal Relations

If admonition by the husband fails to correct the wife, the husband may refuse to share his bed with the wife; that is, he may suspend conjugal relations with her. But this must be confined to a reasonable period of time and should not be continued indefinitely.

3) Light Beating

Muslim jurists have generally discouraged Muslims from beating their wives. However, if a wife's behaviour is against the commandments of Allah and the injunctions of the Prophet (peace be upon him), chastising or beating her in a light manner may become necessary. However, the Prophet has enjoined on the husband not to beat his wife on her face or in such a way that will leave a mark on her body. (It is interesting to note here that a recent study showed that there are about a million men in the United States who silently receive light beatings from their wives!)

If one of these three measures succeeds in correcting the woman and she mends her ways and becomes obedient to her husband, the Qur'an ordains that the husband should not find faults in her in order to annoy, nag, or persecute her.

The relationship between husband and wife is graphically described in the Qur'an:

> **They are a garment to you**
> **and you are a garment to them. (2:187)**

Taken with another verse of the Qur'an which says:

> **The best garment**
> **is the garment of God-consciousness (7:26)**

the importance of this simile can be realised. It requires that a husband and wife should be as garments for each other. Just as garments are for the protection, comfort, show, and concealment of human beings, so Allah expects husbands and wives to be for one another.

Another verse of the Qur'an says:

> **But, in accordance with justice,**
> **the wife's rights (with regard to their husbands)**
> **are equal to the (husband's) rights**
> **with regard to them,**
> **although men are a degree above them.**
> **And Allah is Almighty, Wise. (2:228)**

The statement that men are a degree above women means that authority within the household has been given to the husband in preference to the wife because a heavier burden has been placed on his shoulders by another verse of the Qur'an which says:

**Men shall take full care of women,
because Allah has given the one
more strength than the other,
and because they support them
from their means (4:34)**

A dispassionate look at the relative position of men and women in a Muslim home reveals that a most reasonable and delicate balance has been struck between them and they have been given equally important roles in the creation of a wholesome base to society.

Men are exhorted by Allah to consort with their wives in kindness. They are further told:

**If you dislike something,
Allah might yet make it a source
of abundant good. (4:19)**

In his *khutba* on the Mount of Mercy at Arafat, the Prophet (peace be upon him) emphasised that Muslims should be good and kind towards their wives:

O people! You have rights over your wives as they have rights over you. Your rights over them are that they live chaste lives, and do not admit into their homes anybody whom you dislike, and that they do not fall into manifest evil. If they do, Allah permits you to keep them away from your beds in order that they may improve and mend their ways. You may even resort to such light chastisement as may not produce any harmful effect on their bodies. But in case they do no such thing you are duty-bound to arrange suitably for their food and clothing according to your means. Well, remember! Your treatment of your wives should be righteous and kind, for they are in your custody and cannot safe-guard their rights. The day you married them, you considered them as a trust of Allah, and you brought them home according to His injunctions.

Marriage with a Polytheist (Mushrikah)

It is absolutely forbidden for a Muslim man to marry a polytheist woman whether she is a worshipper of an idol, an animal, a tree, or a stone. The Qur'an commands:

Do not marry women idolators until they believe:

> a slave woman who believes is better
> than an unbelieving woman,
> even though she allures you.
> Unbelievers do but beckon you to the Fire.
> But Allah beckons by His Grace
> to the Garden of bliss and forgiveness,
> and makes His signs clear to mankind
> that they may celebrate His praise. (2:221)

This verse was revealed about a Muslim, Kannaz ibn Hasin al-Ghanawi, who had been attracted to a certain woman polytheist since the days before he entered Islam. She was called Anaq and she asked him to marry her. So he asked the Prophet (peace be upon him) for permission to marry her and Allah revealed this verse and the Prophet told Kannaz that he should not marry her since he was a Muslim while she was a polytheist.[10]

'Abdullah ibn 'Abbas, however, mentions a different reason for the revelation of this verse. According to him, 'Abdullah ibn Rawaha once became angry with his slave-girl and when the Prophet (peace be upon him) asked 'Abdullah b. Rawaha about her, he told the Prophet that she fasted, offered her prayers, made ablution properly, and believed that there was no god but Allah and that he (Muhammad) was the Messenger of Allah. On hearing this, the Prophet told 'Abdullah that she was then a believer. Then 'Abdullah declared her to be a free woman and married her. Many Muslims taunted him for marrying a slave-girl. They did this because they preferred to marry polytheist women of high lineage rather than Muslim slave-girls. It was on this occasion that 'Abdullah's action was approved by Allah through this verse.

If a Muslim woman renounces Islam, she can no longer remain the legally married wife of a Muslim. Therefore her marriage with a Muslim husband becomes null and void immediately she apostasizes.

Not much deliberation is needed to appreciate the rationale of the rule given in verse 221 of *Surah* 2 of the Qur'an prohibiting Muslim men from marrying *mushrik* women. The relations between husband and wife are not merely sexual, but also spiritual and cultural. No doubt it is possible that the Muslim man may influence the polytheist woman and their offspring to become muslim. But it is equally possible that the *mushrik* woman may mislead the Muslim man and their offspring into the ways of *shirk*. The Shari'ah does not countenance taking chances on such a vital matter. It expects a Muslim to avoid a mixture of Islam and non-Islam being bred in his family. A polytheist might approve of this in the name of "liberalism", but a Muslim as a monotheist cannot and should not enter into such a wedlock merely for the sake of gratification of animal lust. He must rather suppress his passions than do anything that might take him or his progeny towards *shirk* and the fire of Hell.

Marriage with a Woman of the Book

Islam considers the Jews and the Christians as 'People of the Book' (*Ahl al-Kitab*) because they believe in the Torah and the Evangil, the Books of Allah revealed to the prophets Musa and 'Isa respectively. Marriage with a woman of the People of the Book (*kitabiyyah*) is permitted in Islam:

> **This day are all things good and pure**
> **made lawful unto you.**
> **The food of the People of the Book**
> **is lawful unto you and yours is lawful unto them.**
> **Lawful unto you in marriage**
> **are not only chaste women who are believers,**
> **but chaste women among the People of the Book**
> **revealed before your time,**
> **when you give them due dowers, and desire chastity**
> **and not lewdness nor secret intrigues. (5:6)**

There is a consensus of opinion among the Sunni schools that marriage with Jewish and Christian women is permitted. It was also the practice of the Companions of the Prophet *(Sahabah)* like 'Uthman, Talha, Ibn 'Abbas, Jabir, and Hudhaifah, and the Followers *(Tabi'un)* like Sa'id ibn al-Musayyib, Sa'id ibn Jubair, Al-Hassan, Mujahid, Tawus, Akramah and others.

However, in spite of this, 'Abdullah ibn 'Umar was of the opinion that a Muslim should not marry a Jewess or a Christian woman. He used to say, "Allah has forbidden us to marry the polytheists, and I do not understand it as being other than manifest polytheism when a woman says that her Lord is 'Isa, when he is a but a servant from the servants of Allah."[11]

Although we also respectfully submit that no doubt some pious

Sahabah and some of the Followers *(Tabi'un)* did marry the *Kitabiyyah* women, yet Muslims of today must think long and deeply before contracting such marriages. The *Sahabah* and *Tabi'un* had exemplary characters and their lives were full of righteousness and piety and even after marrying such women who followed different religions and celebrated different festivals, they knew how to keep their children immune from the influence of their mothers. There is not a single example of the children of the *Sahabah* or the *Tabi'un* embracing the religions of their mothers. But the Muslims of today do not have the necessary strength of character to prevent their non-Muslim wives exercising unwarranted influence over them as well as their children. For example, a Christian woman may sip wine as a part of her religious ritual, and the habit may slowly find its way into the house. Therefore it would be better if the Muslims considered marriage with women of the *Ahl al-Kitab* as *makruh* despite the fact that there is permission to marry them.

In fact certain *'ulama'* have reached the opinion *(ijtihad)* that if the number of Muslim women in a country is too large to be matched by Muslim men, it is considered unlawful for Muslim men to marry the *kitabiyyah* women. No Muslim woman can marry a *kitabi* man, if Muslim men run after *kitabiyyah* women, so how will Muslim women be able to find husbands?

According to the Hanafi school it is not lawful to marry a *kitabiyyah* in the *Dar al-Harb* (Abode of War) because it may become a source of mischief for the reason that the children of such marriage are more likely to be inclined towards the religion of their mother.[12]

The Maliki school, on the other hand, has two opinions. The first is that marriage with *kitabiyyah* is completely disapproved *(makruh)* whether she is a *dhimmi* (protected citizen of *Dar as-Salam* (Abode of Islam)) or from *Dar al-Harb*. Indeed, the disapproval of a woman in the latter category is greater.

The second opinion is that there is no prohibition or absolute disapproval against marrying a *kitabiyyah* because the Qur'an has given tacit approval to such a marriage. However, such a marriage in the *Dar al-Islam* is something to be avoided because a *kitabiyyah* women is likely to drink wine or eat pork or go to church or synagogue for which she has permission under her own religion and this may affect the religious beliefs and behaviour of her children.

It is not essential that both of the parents are of the *Ahl al-Kitab*. It is sufficient if her father is a *kitabi* even though her mother is an idolworshipper. The Shafi'i and Hanbali schools believe that both her parents must be *Ahl al-Kitab* in order to make the marriage of a *kitabiyyah* valid. If her father is a *kitabi* and her mother is an idolworshipper, the marriage is unlawful even though she has reached the age of puberty and has accepted the religion of her father.

Marriage with Sabian and Magian Women

The Sabians are a community which does not have any particular religion. Mujahid, an eminent theologian, considers them as *Ahl al-Kitab* who read the Psalms of David. But Hasan, another theologian, says that they worshipped angels. According to 'Abdu'r-Rahman ibn Zayd, they lived in the vicinity of Mosul and they had no book and no prophet merely saying with their mouths *la ilaha illa'llah* (there is no god but Allah) but not moulding their actions according to it. This is why the polytheists of Makka used to say to the Companions of the Prophet, "These Sabians ressemble us in saying *la ilaha illa'llah* ."

According to Ibn Kathir, the famous commentator on the Qur'an, the Sabians lived in the vicinity of Iraq, knew Allah, had their own Shari'ah, believed in some Prophets, fasted for thirty days in a year, and even prayed five times a day but not in the direction of the Ka'ba.[13]

The Holy Qur'an mentions the Sabians, in the following words:

> **Those who believe (in the Qur'an),**
> **those who follow the Jewish (Scriptures),**
> **and the Sabians and the Christians,**
> **and those who believe in Allah and the Last Day,**
> **and work righteousness,**
> **on them shall be no fear,**
> **nor shall they grieve. (5:72)**

It is on these grounds that a Muslim is permitted to marry a Sabian woman.

Allamah Yusuf 'Ali, the well-known translator of the Qur'an, has ventured to use the term Sabian to cover the followers of

Buddha, Confucius or the Vedas. But it is respectfully submitted that because no cogent and convincing reason has been given by the Allamah to justify such extension, it is not easy for this author to agree with him, particularly when the question of the validity of the marriage of a Muslim man with a Hindu, Buddhist, or Shinto woman comes up for consideration. It is submitted that the women of these faiths should be regarded as on a par with polytheists.

Magians or Zoroastrians or Parsees are those who worship fire. Marriage with a Zoroastrian woman is not forbidden to a Muslim. It is also lawful for a Muslim to eat the meat of animals slaughtered by them. But strictly speaking, they are not *Ahl al-Kitab* because they have no Book. In fact, they do not believe in prophethood. Imam ash-Shafi'i narrates that the khalif, 'Umar, once said, "I do not know how I should treat the Magians." 'Abdur-Rahman ibn 'Awf, a famous Companion of the Prophet, advised him that he had heard the Messenger of Allah saying that they should be treated in the same way as *Ahl al-Kitab*.

Ban on Muslim Women Marrying Non-Muslims
The Qur'an absolutely prohibits a Muslim woman from marrying a non-Muslim, even if he happens to be one of the *Ahl al-Kitab*. It declares:

> O you who believe,
> when there come to you
> believing women refugees,
> examine (and test) them.
> Allah knows best as to their faith.
> If you ascertain that they are believers,
> then do not send them back to the unbelievers.
> They are not lawful (wives) for the unbelievers,
> nor are the unbelievers their lawful husbands. (60:10)

According to this verse, when a woman leaves her home on account of her belief in Allah and her love for Islam and the Holy Prophet and comes to the believers and they realise that she is a believer, they must not, under any circumstances, send her back to the unbelievers. The rationale of this rule is that unbelievers can never treat the believing women in marriage according to the principle of 'commanding to the good' *(amr bi'l-ma'ruf)* and so no

Muslim woman should ever marry a non-Muslim.

Solemnising a Muslim Marriage

According to the Maliki school, there are five requirements for a Muslim marriage:

(i) The guardian must give his consent to the marriage.

(ii) The bridegroom must be competent to marry.

(iii) The bride must also be competent to marry and should be neither in *'iddah* nor in the state of *ihram*.

(iv) There should be *sighah* i.e. *ijab* (the proposal) and *qabul* (the acceptance).

(v) The dowry must be agreed.

The Shafi'i school also insists upon requirements (i) to (iv) of the Maliki school, but it also requires that the *sighah (ijab* and *qabul)* should take place in the presence of two witnesses. The dowry should be agreed, but if it is is not agreed the marriage will be valid and the dowry will be determined by the court.

The Hanafi school regards only the *sighah* as essential to marriage. Other requirements, as in the Maliki and Shafi'i school, may be satisfied, but they are not essential and may be dispensed with. In *sighah* (i.e. *ijab* and *qabul*) clear words must be used. *Qabul* must be made in the same meeting where *ijab* is uttered *(fi majlis al-ijab)*.

It is *mustahab* (commendable) to give a *khutbah* (sermon) before the marriage rites are performed. This may provide an opportunity for informing and advising the bride and bridegroom of their marital responsibilities in Islam and it may be long or short as the occasion demands. The shortest recommended form of *khutbah* is just to say: "Praise be to Allah and blessings and salutations be on the Messenger of Allah. The Prophet (peace be upon him) used to recite the following three verses of the Qur'an on the occasion of the solemnisation of a marriage:

O you who believe, fear Allah as He should be feared, and do not die except in a state of Islam (3:102)

**O mankind, fear your Lord
who created you from a single person,
and created of like nature, his mate,
and from those two scattered**

countless men and women like seeds.
Fear Allah, through whom
you demand your mutual rights,
and respect the wombs (that bore you),
for Allah ever watches over you. (4:1)

O you who believe, fear Allah
and always say a word directed to the right,
that He may make your conduct whole and sound
and forgive you your sins.
He that obeys Allah and His Messenger
has already attained
the highest achievements. (33:71-72)

The Prophet (peace be upon him) also used to make a short *du'a* (supplication) after the solemnisation of a marriage. One of his prayers was as follows:

"May Allah bless you and may blessings be upon you and may your coming together be auspicious."

It was strongly recommended by the Prophet that the bridegroom should host a *walimah* (marriage feast) for friends and well-wishers on the day following the marriage. All schools of Islamic law regard this practice as *sunna al-mu'akkadah* (a binding sunna). But there should be no extravagance in the feast which must be as simple as possible.

4
POLYGAMY: A MISUNDERSTOOD PHENOMENON

Wars and natural disasters may sometimes cause an appreciable decline in the number of men in society as compared with the number of women, for the reason that men take greater risks on such occasions as soldiers and fighters. Such events may leave countless women without any home or help. Either such women may be left alone to fend for themselves or they may be provided with the security of a home and protection. The Shari'ah prefers the second course. Since it aims at the establishment of a pious, just, and morally strong society, it does not tolerate any woman seeking refuge under the roof of any man unless she is married to him or he is within the prohibited degrees of relationship to her.

In such a situation polygamy seems the only reasonable alternative to meet the needs of women for protection and care. However, there is no compulsion on any woman. If a woman feels that she can secure her peace, comfort, and happiness from others without seeking help or protection, no-one can compel her to marry a man who is already the husband of another woman. Thus polygamy is a sort of remedial law in Islam which a person may use only if they so desire.

Polygamy and the Qur'an and the Sunnah

Before the advent of Islam polygamy was practised by the pagan Arabs without any check or limits. The result was oppression and injustice for all wives. Islam sought to remedy this situation and laid down that a maximum of four wives might be taken by a man at one time, and then only when he possessed the strength of character to deal justly with them. The only Qur'anic verse that refers to polygamy is as follows:

"If you fear that you will not be able
to deal justly with the orphans,
marry the women of your choice,
two or three or four.

**But if you fear that you will not be able
to deal justly with them, then only one." (4:3)**

The above rule on polygamy was introduced conditionally. The verse especially refers to the justice to be done to orphans. It was revealed immediately after the Battle of Uhud when the Muslim community was left with many orphans and widows and some captives-of-war. The treatment was to be governed by principles of greatest humanity and equality. As Yusuf 'Ali says: "The occasion is past but the principles remain. Marry the orphans if you are quite sure that is the way to protect their interests and their property with perfect justice to them and to your own dependants, if you have any"

The verse was not merely limited to orphans, but has a general application with regard to the marriage laws in Islam. The Muslim jurists, therefore, have laid down the following conditions if someone wants to take more than one wife:

(i) He should have sufficient financial resources to look after the needs of the additional wives that he has taken.

(ii) He must do equal justice to them all. Each wife should be treated equally as far as the fulfilment of their conjugal and other rights is concerned.

If a man feels that he will not be able to treat another wife with equality and justice or he does not have the means to support another wife, he should restrict himself to marrying only one wife. Imam Malik says in *al-Muwatta'* that when Ghaylan ibn Salamah accepted Islam he had ten wives. The Messenger of Allah (peace be upon him) said, "Keep four of them and set the others free."

Similarly Abu Da'ud mentions from Harith, "I accepted Islam and I had eight wives. I mentioned this to the Prophet and he told me to choose four of them."

If a man takes more than one wife it is absolutely essential for him to be as just as possible between them. The very object of marriage in Islam is to have a healthy family where a man and his wife or wives and children live in peace, love, and harmony, as is required by the injunction of the Qur'an:

**Among His signs
is that He created for you mates
from among yourselves**

**that you may dwell in tranquillity with them,
and He has put love and mercy
between your hearts. (30:20)**

Thus the man as the father and the woman as the mother of the children dwell together and bring up a family unit. Different people have different temperaments and feelings, but if kindness, love, tenderness, and tranquillity can be maintained, such a family is successful. If this is not possible, then one must limit oneself to what one can easily manage, that is, one wife.

The following situations will allow polygamy as the best solution:

(i) When the wife is suffering from a serious disease like paralysis, epilepsy or a contagious disease. In these circumstances it would be better if there were another wife to look after the needs of the husband and children. Her presence will also help the sickly wife.

(ii) When the wife proves barren and after medical examination the experts have given their opinion that she is not capable of bearing a child. The husband then should marry a second wife so that he may have children since a child is one of the joys of this life.

(iii) When she is of unsound mind. In that case the husband and children will suffer a great deal.

(iv) When the woman has reached old age and has become weak and infirm and cannot look after the house and property of the husband.

(v) When the husband finds that his wife has a bad character and cannot be reformed. He should then have another wife.

(vi) When she has moved way from the husband's house and has become disobedient and the husband finds it difficult to reform her. He should then take another wife.

(vii) During a period of war when men are killed and women are left behind in large numbers, polygamy can provide the best solution.

(viii) Apart from the above circumstances, if the man feels that he cannot do without a second wife in order to satisfy his natural desire in the case of it being very strong and when he has enough means to support her, he should take another wife. There are certain areas in the world where people are physically very virile and cannot be satisfied with one wife. In such cases polygamy can provide an answer.

Only Limited Polygamy Allowed

Islam limited the limitless polygamy practised in the *Jahiliyyah* society of Arabs and non-Arabs. It was a fashion with chiefs of tribes and rulers to keep big harems. Even some Muslim rulers became victims of passion and practised limitless polygamy in the later periods of Islamic history. Whatever their practise, such polygamy has no place in Islam. If necessary a Muslim can marry up to four wives and no more at a given time. According to Imam ash-Shafi'i, it is not lawful for anyone other than the Prophet to marry more than four wives at a given time.[1]

Some of the Zahirites maintain that the Qur'anic words, *mathna* means "two, two", and *thulath* "three, three" and Ruba' "four, four" and thus the number permitted swells to eighteen. There are some who think erroneously that "*Mathna wa thulatha wa ruba'*" put together come up to nine and so nine wives are allowed in Islam, This is, in reality, an incorrect interpretation of this Qur'anic injunction. The Prophetic interpretation of this verse is contained in the following *hadith* of the Prophet.

The Prophet said to Ghaylan ibn Umayyah al-Thaqafi who had just accepted Islam and had ten wives, "Choose four of them and give up all others." [2]

Once a Muslim marries more than one wife, it is essential for him to treat them equally in matters of food, residence, clothing and even in sexual relationship as much as possible. If someone is a little doubtful in showing equal treatment in fulfilling his wives' rights, he must not take more. If he feels able to fulfil his responsibilities to only one, he should not marry two. If he can do justice to only two, he should not marry three. The final limit is that of four wives.

> **If you fear**
> **that you will not be able to do justice,**
> **then marry only one. (4:3)**

The justice referred to in this verse only relates to equitable treatment as far as it is humanly possible. In the matter of love, even if a man sincerely purposes to do equal justice, he will not be able to since human beings are what they are.

The Qur'an refers to this human weakness in the following words:

> You will never be able
> to be fair and just between women,
> even if it is your ardent desire,
> but do not turn away from a woman altogether
> so as to leave her as it were
> hanging in the air. (4:129)

Shaikh Muhammad ibn Sirin, explaining this verse, said that the inability referred to in the Holy Qur'an is in respect of love and sexual intercourse. Shaikh Abu Bakr ibn al-'Arabi says, "No one can control his heart since it is entirely in the hands of Allah." The same is the case with cohabitation when one may satisfy one wife better than another. Since this was not the intention of the man, it is not his fault and hence he will not be held responsible.

The Mother of the Faithful, 'A'ishah, reported from the Prophet saying, "The Messenger of Allah used to distribute things and do justice to all and used to say, 'My God, this is my distribution of what is in my control but I have no responsibility for what is in Your control and over which I have no control.' " (Abu Da'ud, at-Tirmidhi, and an-Nisa'i.)

When the *hadith* speaks of "the thing under Allah's control" the reference is to the heart and matters connected to the heart. After understanding the matter of equal justice to one's wives, the following *hadith* of the Prophet must be kept in mind in order to avoid excesses. The Holy Prophet said:

"A man who marries more than one woman and then does not deal justly with them, will be resurrected with half his faculties paralysed."

Preservation of the higher values and the promotion of righteousness must be the constant objective. Permission to marry more than one woman at a time is a necessary emergency provision for the preservation of high social values and for safeguarding society against promiscuity.

At this stage it becomes relevant to quote Billy Graham on polygamy: "If Christianity cannot do so, it is to its detriment. Islam has permitted polygamy as a solution to social ills and has allowed a certain degree of latitude to human nature, but only strictly within the framework of the law. Christian countries make a great show of monogamy, but actually they practise polygamy. No one is unaware of the part mistresses play in society. In this respect, Islam is a fundamentally honest religion and permits a Muslim to marry a second wife if he must, but strictly forbids all clandestine amatory associations in order to safeguard the moral probity of the community."

Modernist Approach to Polygamy

There is a growing tendency to consider some Islamic institutions to be outmoded when, according to some modernists, they do not conform to the western pattern of life. This is particularly true in the case of polygamy which some scholars have vehemently opposed. They have even tried to misinterpret certain verses of the Qur'an, saying that polygamy is not allowed in Islam. The two verses of the Qur'an they have referred to to strengthen their argument are verse 3 and verse 129 of *Surat an-Nisa'* (Chapter 4 of the Qur'an). Verse 3 reads:

> **If you fear that you will not be able**
> **to deal justly with the orphans,**
> **marry women of your choice, two or three or four;**
> **but if you fear that you will not be able**
> **to deal justly with them, then only one.**

Verse 129 reads:

> **You will never be able to be fair**
> **and just between women,**
> **even if it is your ardent desire.**

The argument usually tendered in respect of the above two verses is that Islam has allowed marrying more than one wife on the condition that the man be perfectly fair and just to all his wives. But this condition is almost impossible to fulfil as is mentioned in verse 129 quoted above. Hence they argue that polygamy is not allowed in Islam because a man who marries more than one wife puts himself in an impossible situation.

The modernists consider verse 129 as a legal condition attached to polygamous unions. Since impartial treatment is impossible, one must restrict oneself to monogamy. What they overlook is the fact that "impartial treatment" in the matter of residence, food and clothing is a relative term which will differ from person to person and from country to country according to the economic standards of the society. What one would need to provide in an European country in terms of food, clothing and residence would not apply in certain countries in Asia and Africa where the standard and the cost of living are much lower. Hence it is a matter of conscience for individual husbands to provide his wives equal treatment according to his situation.

Even in one given society the standards would differ - a business man will provide for his wives according to his standard while a labourer, whose income is low, may provide according to his own level of income. The woman that the labourer would marry would be used to a lower standard than the wife of a business man. Besides, wives might voluntarily accept a lower standard and live perfectly happily as happens in many polygamous homes in Africa.

The impact of the colonial era on Muslim countries was so great that they changed their marital laws and imposed restrictions on a husband marrying more than one wife. The first attempt of this kind was made by Syria in 1953. Syrian Law on Personal Status (Decree No. 59) of 1953 provides: ".....the judge is empowered to refuse permission to a married man to marry another woman if it is established that he is not in a position to support two wives..." (Art. 17) Here it was stipulated that men could not to take additional wives unless they were financially capable of duly supporting them.[3] In this case the Syrian jurists, trained in western countries, maintained that the Qur'anic provision in verse 3 of *Surat an-Nisa'* should be regarded as a positive legal condition precedent to the exercise of polygamy and enforced as such by the courts on the principle that those doors that might lead to abuses must be closed.

They made it essential for an intending husband to seek permission of the court to marry. It was required by Article 17 of the law that the *Qadi* could withhold permission from a man who was already married to marry a second wife where it was established that he was not in a position to support both of them. Defaulters would be considered to be liable to penalties and the court would not recognize the marriage, although in spite of the penalty clause they did not go so far as declaring the marriage invalid.

In Tunisia, polygamy was prohibited outright by the law of personal status in 1957. The Tunisian Code of Personal Status, 1957, says: "Polygamy is forbidden. Any person who, having entered into a bond of marriage, contracts another marriage before the dissolution of the preceding one, is liable to one year's imprisonment and to a fine..." (Art. 18) Here too, modern jurists, influenced by the Western pattern of life, declared that the Qur'anic verse 3 of *Surat an-Nisa'* would not be construed strictly as a moral exhortation but as a legal condition precedent to polygamy, and therefore, no second marriage should be permissible unless and until adequate evidence was forthcoming that the wives be would treated impartially. Since they thought that in modern social and economic conditions such impartial treatment was virtually an impossibility, they maintained that the essential conditions of polygamy were impossible to fulfil. In other words, the Tunisian jurists even went a step further and completely prohibited polygamy against the explicit Qur'anic provision.

The Moroccan Code of 1958 took a middle course and prohibited polygamy conditionally when there was any apprehension of unequal treatment. The Moroccan Code of Personal Status, 1958, says, "Polygamy is prohibited where it is likely to involve injustice towards the wives...The marriage contract concerning the second wife shall not be drawn up until the latter has been informed that her prospective spouse is already married." (Art. 30) The courts were only allowed to intervene by granting divorce on the grounds of unequal treatment which is not that much of a departure from the Maliki school of jurisprudence which is practised in Morocco and which allows a co-wife to claim divorce if she is not given proper maintenance.

Similarly in Iraq, the Law of Personal Status of 1959 did not declare polygamy as prohibited, but imposed restrictions on the institution. The Iraqi Code on Personal Status, 1959, reads, "....it is not permissible to marry more than one woman without authorization from the Judge. The grant of permission is regulated by the conditions that the husband's financial status permits his supporting the wives and that it is for a genuine benefit." (Art. 3) One could not marry a second wife without the permission of the *Qadi* who would not grant permission unless he was satisfied that the husband was financially capable of supporting an additional wife and that some lawful benefit for the husband was found in such a marriage. The *Qadi* would not give permission unless he was satisfied that there was no fear of any unequal treatment of the wives.

In Pakistan, restriction was placed on polygamous marriage by the Muslim Family Law Ordinance of 1961 which requires that writ-

ten permission from the Arbitration Council was required before one
could marry a second wife. Pakistan's Family Law Ordinance provides, "No man, during the subsistence of an existing marriage,
shall, except with the previous permission in writing of the
Arbitration Council, contract another marriage..." (Sect.
6) Permission would only be granted if the Arbitration Council was
satisfied that the proposed marriage was necessary and just. In this
case the consent of the existing wife was required except in cases of
insanity, physical infirmity or sterility. But in any case the Council's
permission was essential before the contraction of a second marriage. The defaulter was liable to be imprisoned up to one year or
would have to pay a fine up to Rs5000 or both. If the *mahr* was
deferred, he was required to pay it forthwith and the existing wife
had the right to get a divorce. In spite of all these restrictions, if a
second marriage was contracted without the Council's permission, it
would not be considered legally invalid.

The above examples lead us naturally to a consideration of the
conflict between the Qur'anic injunctions and the so-called reforms
in respect of polygamy in certain Muslim countries. There are countries where the Shari'ah Law of polygamy has not been tampered
with by modernist forces, like Saudi Arabia, most countries in East
and West Africa, and in Asia. Then there are countries like Syria
and Tunisia where polygamy, obviously allowed in the Qur'an and
the *Sunnah*, has been prohibited by law. There are some other countries where serious restrictions have been imposed by law on contracting a second marriage, but the marriage, if it takes place, is not
rendered invalid.

It is interesting to note that these law reforms in Muslim countries are of recent origin, since it was first introduced in Syria in
1952 and later some other Muslim countries followed suit. It is my
candid view that the countries which have prohibited polygamy by
law have gone against the injunction of the Qur'an and the *Sunnah*
of the Prophet and the practice of the *Tabi'un* and the *Tabi'u't-
Tabi'un.*

It should be borne in mind that the role of the Prophet did not
end with an announcement of the *sunnah* , or the way of life, to the
world at large. He had to guide the people who followed him,
explaining to them the implications of all approved actions, the
moral code, the divine injunctions and the form of law that sustains
the entire system. If polygamy were not allowed, he would have

stopped people practising it in his lifetime. They are a number of *ahadith* of the Prophet in which cases from polygamous homes were brought to him. Solutions were found and justice was done, and in some cases marriages were dissolved if they became unworkable. But there is not a single *hadith* that suggests that polygamy was forbidden by the Prophet or the *Rashidun* Khalifs or Muslim rulers of the Umayyad and 'Abbasid dynasties. This brings up the important question of the role of *'ulama'* and *fuqaha'* of Islam, the great learned men and jurists who have guided the *ummah* since the death of the Prophet. The founders and leaders of the four schools of Islamic jurisprudence and their disciples have left behind volumes of of their works. They too have tried to find solutions to the problems arising out of polygamous unions, but have never prohibited polygamy outright. Why did the great *'ulama'* have to wait for 1400 years until 1953 to pronounce their prohibition of polygamy?

By declaring this prohibition, the so-called modernist reformers have refused to accept the Qur'anic injunction and have indirectly rejected the *sunnah* of the Prophet by declaring it unworkable and have also disregarded the opinions of the pious *'ulama'*.

More than thirty years have passed since polygamy was banned in some Muslim countries. Much has been written in appreciation of these reformers by European scholars. The existence of such reforms are cited as a factor which makes people more cautious in contracting second marriages. If one takes the statistics of polygamous marriages before and after the prohibition in Syria and Tunisia, one would find a few cases where people have refrained from contracting a second marriage. But at the same time it has heightened the tensions in the minds of those who were capable both economically and physically of marrying and satisfying more wives. A few have married contrary to the law and undergone penalties, but many have taken a short cut of entering into extra-marital relationships secretly, aping the life-style of the Western world in order to cling to monogamy.

There is a dearth of empirical evidence which might enable us to answer the crucial question: has the prohibition of polygamy served as a deterrent? Has Muslim society become more prosperous because of this prohibition? Quite naturally, empirical evidence in this field will remain unobtainable. It is common-place to say that the imaginary fear of the misuse of polygamy is widespread and abiding in the minds of western-trained Muslim elites. The question

is whether such fear, even if justified to some extent knowing the
unpredictability of human nature, will remain when we think of the
alternative, i.e. importing the moral vices of Western culture.
Knowing how human beings are, even the provisions of marriage,
divorce, trade and commerce and all other aspects of law stand to be
misused.

As for those Muslim countries which have imposed heavy fines
and imprisonment (or both) for one whose does not first obtain permission from the Arbitration Council as in Pakistan or an authorization from the Judge as in Morocco, here too there is an obvious vio-
lation of the Shari'ah provision on polygamy. Permission will only
be granted if the existing wife gives her consent except in cases of
insanity, physical infirmity or sterility. Obliging the man to justify
his intention by giving convincing reasons would give the
Arbitration Council or Courts far more powers of restraining even
necessary polygamy. Some women tend to be very jealous by nature
and in spite of the fact that the husband needs a second wife on con-
ditional grounds, a woman of this kind will not understand her husband nor would the court understand the man's needs easily since
"one would have great difficulty in explaining, biologically, such a
sudden change of heart"[4] If a man's legitimate biological desires are
suppressed against his will, it will give rise to adultery, concubinage
and prostitution. The best course open for Muslims, therefore, is to
act according to the advice of the Qur'an:

**So take what the Apostle assigns to you,
and deny yourself that which he withholds from you. (59.7)**

The *Ummah* has lived successfully for fourteen hundred years
without these reforms, and it can, *insha'llah*, survive the future.

Polygamy: a Sociological Issue in Africa

The main purpose of marriage in the mind of an African man is
the production of children who are his glory. If children do not
come, or do not come fast enough, as the result of a marriage, the
man increases the number of his wives although he does not divorce
his barren wife. In traditional African society, the number of a
man's wives and children was the measure of his success in life and
the children were considered their father's assurance of protection
and support in his old age. The possession of many wives and chil-

dren was regarded as a sign of wealth and nobility. It was not unknown for a man to have as many as 200 children.

Polygamy is an old established custom and to the African it appears not only a reasonable but almost an essential institution. In Iboland in Nigeria in West Africa, it is traditionally obligatory on a father to marry the first wife for his sons. The sons in turn are expected to marry an additional one, two or three wives for themselves. Otherwise they will be regarded as weaklings among their age group and in the community. Even their wives do not object to the addition of other women in the life of their husbands; they believe that extra hands lighten the work in the house and on the farm.

Most Africans feel that monogamy is an institution brought by the Christian missionaries, seeing it as a part of European culture imposed on the newly-converted Africans by the missionaries. Thus, monogamy is nowadays regarded as a foreign institution while polygamy is accepted as being traditional. It is not surprising, therefore, that some African writers who have chosen the clash of cultures as a main theme in their novels, T.M. Aluko as an obvious example, see Christianity as a "one man, one wife" religion. It can be clearly seen that polygamy has all along been a traditional African institution which is up till now warmly embraced by the Africans not only for religious but also for socio-economic reasons.

When the Christian missions began their work of evangelisation, it was extremely difficult for the missionaries to admit certain essentially African aspects such as the permissive attitude towards polygamy in the face of the official policy that had been laid down in this respect. If a Christian became polygamous, he was excommunicated from the church.

In 1888, for example, the first authoritative Anglican ruling on the subject was given at the Lambeth Conference when it was decided that a polygamist might be received as a catechumen "but should not be baptised, though the wives of polygamists might be admitted."[5] In the early stages, the Christian missionary churches were of the opinion that polygamists who had entered into their matrimonial engagements before knowing the Christian demand in marriage should not be asked to dissolve all of them save one, but admitted to baptism as they were. This was a view at variance with the almost universal practice. A woman married to a polygamist was usually permitted to become a communicant, provided that she married him before her conversion.

The Bishop of Lagos issued the Diocesan Directions in 1948 saying that "...the wives of polygamists need not be excluded provided the alliance was entered into when they, the wives, were in a state of ignorance...The wives of a polygamist who knowingly and with full understanding entered into marriage with their husbands after baptism cannot be admitted to Confirmation or Holy Communion."[6] As for baptism of children not born in Holy Wedlock, the Archbishop of West Africa has permitted that they "need not be denied the sacrament of baptism, but due and proper provision must be made for their Christian upbringing; and godparents must be chosen who are in full communion with the church."[7]

This liberal view is now applicable to the children of polygamists with the further advice from the Archbishop that in the case of a female child, baptism should be postponed, except in case of emergency, until the child comes to years of discretion and can answer for herself; unless the father has a real interest in and an understanding of the church, and is prepared to recognise the church's rule about marriage as far as his daughter is concerned and agrees not to give her in marriage to a polygamist. The 1938 meeting of the International Missionary Council at Tambaram sums up the Christian attitude towards polygamy: "The Church must maintain its insistence on monogamy. This is not a matter to be settled by the individual conscience - the criterion is the Will of God for the people whom He has redeemed and purified in Christ. Monogamy is not a mere factor of civilization; it is vital to the life of the Church, and its value has been realized in its own experience; it was taught by the Lord Himself and has scriptural authority behind it."

Evidence shows, however, that nowadays these rulings are not strictly adhered to, especially as far as the Anglican denomination is concerned. Some staunch members of this denomination are said to be polygamists and nothing has been done to eject them from the fold. Their wives are not denied the opportunity of being full members of the fold, although the official ruling has not yet been changed. Some questions are bound to arise at this juncture. Are the rulings of 1888 now outdated? Do they need a review?

The Prophetic counsel is quite clear in the matter and stipulates detailed regulations and instructions for a polygamists subjecting him to a severe discipline. The Prophet has said, "A man who mar-

ries more than one woman and then does not deal justly with them
will be resurrected with half his faculties paralysed."

According to Islam, it is essential to preserve higher values and
promote righteousness. Therefore, permission to marry more than
one woman at a time is a necessary provision in order to preserve
and foster high social values and to safeguard society against
promiscuity. This is the reason why permission for polygamy may
be availed of in a national or or domestic emergency, or where circumstances make it desirable that the ordinary rule of monogamy
be departed from (in case of increase in the number of women's
population).

Permission for polygamy has undoubtedly been abused by some
Muslims in many parts of the world. More often than not, it has
been practised merely to satisfy the appetites or in accordance with
a tradition of marrying more than one, "according to Yoruba tradition", and not according to religion.

Answers to a questionnaire which we circulated in a sample survey in Ife-Ife classified the reasons offered by Christian and Muslim
household heads when asked about their attitude towards polygamy.
An appreciable number of people interviewed replied to this question. The vast majority, however, replied "yes" or "no" without giving any reasons whatsoever. The answers confirm the view
expressed by Trimingham that whilst all West Africans allow
polygamy, its practice is restricted by such factors as wealth and
women's role in family and economic life.[8] About nine percent of all
Muslims interviewed expressed disapproval of polygamy. It seems,
however, that in the present state of affairs there are more Christians
who are polygamous than Muslims.

There is no doubt that the Church authorities are aware of the
fact that there are polygamists within its fold. It can be suggested
that the Church, still remembering the clash which ensued between
Christianity and the traditional African institutions when missionary
activities were at their embryonic stage, is trying to avoid divisions
within its congregation. Since society changes with time, it may be
that all they are trying to do is to cater for both the spiritual and the
social needs of their people.

The Catholic Church is still very strict about monogamy being
practised by its members. Polygamy is strictly forbidden.
Polygamists cannot be baptized until they have renounced all their
wives, leaving only one. Their wives cannot receive baptism as long

as they are with them. As far as the Catholic Church is concerned, these women are not housewives in the real sense of the term, but concubines, so they are deprived of the opportunity of receiving the Holy Sacraments which practising Catholics enjoy. They are denied Christian burial and their thanksgiving offerings are rejected.

There is no doubt that the Catholic denomination takes very strict measures to see that polygamy is totally extirpated from its fold. It maintains that its members should be nothing but monogamist. It has, however, been realised that every year the Catholic Church loses some of its members who cannot endure monogamy. They see no reason why they should be deprived of their tradition and so they leave the Catholic Church for those Protestant Churches and the "Aladura" Church of the Lord which seem to be silent over the issue of polygamy.

As far as Muslims are concerned, polygamy is permitted by Islam but the right should be exercised under exceptional circumstances. Although Islam permits a plurality of wives, not exceeding four, it is only on condition of strict equality of treatment among them. The Qur'an says:

**If you fear you will not be able
to deal justly with them,
then marry only one. (4:4)**

If a Muslim marries more than one wife, his treatment of each must be absolutely equal. It will be his duty to make identical provision for each wife and her children and spend the same period of time with each.

This also confirms what Dr Driesen[9] has gathered from a number of Muslims in the Ife Division who happened to be monogamous in spite of the fact that they were financially in a position to marry more than one wife.

Polygamy in Africa is a sociological rather than a religious matter; it results more from conformity to the African social pattern than from religious dogma. We have not come across any example during our research of a man actually becoming a Muslim simply because he wanted to be a polygamist.

One may quote the example of the Apostolic Church which is supposedly monogamous but has a high percentage of polygamous followers. When the African Church broke away and later declared that its followers could be polygamous if they so desired, the consequences were not as expected. Indeed, quite the opposite situation resulted and a monogamous section of their followers reverted to their original church.[10] In other words, it is immaterial whether one is a Christian, Muslim or a member of an African church, polygamy is an established attitude and is not a religious question but a traditional and sociological one. Looking at the table of percentages of Churches approving polygamy, it might be interesting to examine some of the reasons given for approval of polygamy. It is clear that polygamy has a high prestige value. A member of the Roman Catholic Church clearly regarded polygamy as a sign of prestige and wealth when he said, "It is a pride to have many wives in my compound." Another person interviewed said that he practised polygamy "because having many wives showed high prestige among his neighbours" and a third considered more wives "a sign of wealth". Some members of the Anglican Church were also interviewed. They had thirty wives, twenty-five wives, and fifteen wives respectively, while an Anglican in communion had ten wives. Another Anglican who was not in communion said he had married fifteen wives because "he had complied with his father's attitude" since his father had up to fifty wives.

Another Christian commented on his attitude to polygamy that it depended upon his ability to marry. A member of an Apostolic Church who consulted an *alfa*[11] instead of a priest said "a Christian might marry about four wives". This was perhaps due to Islamic influence on some Christians. In Yorubaland, Muslims and Christians of all denominations, as well as the followers of the traditional Yoruba religion, live together in perfect harmony and in a number of cases under the same roof. Therefore, it is not surprising if such syncretic elements are discovered in the belief and practice of the Yoruba people. There were some Muslims who declared that they were not obliged to limit themselves to four wives and thought that one should marry "as many as possible". This indicates that even for the Muslims, polygamy is not a religious affair so much as a traditional practice.

Most of the reasons given for polygamy were not religious. Thus some Muslims were opposed to it, and those who practised it did not justify it on the basis of the Qur'an or the *Sunnah* and often mentioned that they married more wives "according to the Yoruba custom".

Some people practising polygamy were motivated by purely

economic reasons and married more wives "according to money to
maintain them," and there were some others who wanted more wives
so that they could help them on their farms. There were a number of
cases in which people married more than one wife because "the first
one did not serve better". In other words, the secondary purpose of
customary marriage among the Yoruba in general and the Ife in particular has always been "to have a woman who would be an assis-
tant to look after the household and lend a helping hand in the work
on the husband's farm". This latter reason largely accounts for the
multiplicity of wives married under customary law in Ife. The more
wives a man has the greater the number of helpers he has on his
farm.[12] Even today the idea of plurality of wives is considered a
necessity among a large number of young men in Ife Division.

Polygamy among Non-Muslims
     There is a popular notion prevalent all over the world that
Muslims are always polygamous. In some countries, where
Muslims are a minority, researches have shown that non-Muslims
are more polygamous than Muslims. In his excellent case-study,
Muslims less polygamous than non-Muslims, Arshad Masood has
provided census figures in tabular form quoting figures from 1910 to
1960. He has successfully shown that non-Muslims, particularly
Hindus, Buddhists and Jainists, who are prohibited from the practice
of polygamy by their religion, tend to be more polygamous than the
Muslims. Arshad Masood writes,[13] "Writing in 1922 in his book
*The Spirit of Islam,*the great Indian jurist, Mr. Justice Syed Ameer
Ali had estimated that 95 out of every 100 Muslims (in India) were
monogamists. The estimate was probably made after taking into
consideration three factors:
(1) Muslim males were more in number than Muslim females;
(2) Muslims in general were not economically well-off; and
(3) Muslims sometimes provided against polygamy by a special
clause in the marriage-deed.
     But many refused to take the statement except with a pinch of
salt. Their own logic suggested to them that Muslim males being
"free" under their religion to have four wives at a time, most of
them and not just five percent must have been maintaining harems.
But a recent report from the office of the Registrar-General and
Census Commissioner of India, New Delhi, not only confirms the
statement of Syed Ameer Ali but also shows that the Muslims are

indeed less polygamous than non-Muslims. This 269 page report is entitled *Polygamous Marriages in India - A Survey* (Census of India 1971, Miscellaneous Studies, Monograph No 4: 1961 Series). It contains an Introduction dated 17th April 1975 by Dr B.K. Burman, Deputy Registrar-General, India (Social Studies Division) and three Tables as follows:

TABLE ONE

A statement giving the break-down of the total number of marriages by the religion of the husband and the time when the marriages took place is given below.

Religion	All period	Before 1910	Between 1911-20	Between 1921-30	Between 1931-40	Between 1941-50	Between 1951-60	Period not stated
Hindu	98,847	3,032	5,463	9,695	13,944	20,659	24,659	2,000
Buddhist	1,166	29	64	113	201	281	332	146
Jain	119	5	8	14	22	24	45	1
Tribal	1,999	26	96	173	346	479	723	156
Others	3,962	121	251	519	717	989	1,267	101
All non-Muslims*	86,096	3,213	5,892	10,574	15,230	21,817	27,026	2,404
Muslims	13,361	400	820	1,605	2,440	3,710	4,224	162
Grand Total	99,457	3,613	6,712	12,119	17,670	25,527	31,250	2,566

* Total of 5 preceding figures supplied by this writer.

TABLE TWO

Altogether 5,911 marriages in the sample are polygamous. A statement giving the break-down of this number by religion and the time when the marriages had taken place is furnished below:

Religion	All period	Before 1910	Between 1911-20	Between 1921-30	Between 1931-40	Between 1941-50	Between 1951-60	Period not stated
Hindu	4,574	83	249	539	947	1,435	1,249	72
Buddhist	93	2	7	9	17	27	27	4
Jain	8	-	-	1	3	1	2	1
Tribal	305	-	8	15	33	84	130	35
Others	168	5	6	27	38	47	44	1
All non-Muslims*	5,146	90	260	581	1,038	1,593	5,951	113
Muslims	765	18	39	83	178	262	182	3
Grand Total	5,911	108	309	674	1,266	1,855	1,634	116

* Total of 5 preceding figures supplied by this writer.

TABLE THREE

A statement giving the trend of incidence by percentage of polygamous marriages among Hindus, Jains, Buddhists, Tribals as separate groups, all non-Muslims taken together and Muslims is given below:

Religion	All period	Before 1910	Between 1911-20	Between 1921-30	Between 1931-40	Between 1941-50	Between 1951-60	Period not stated
Hindu	5.80	2.73	4.54	5.55	6.79	7.15	5.06	3.60
Buddhist	7.97	6.89	10.93	7.96	8.45	9.61	8.13	2.73
Jain	6.72	-	-	7.14	13.63	4.16	4.44	100.00
Tribals	15.25	-	8.33	8.67	9.53	17.53	17.98	22.43
All non-Muslims*	5.98	2.80	4.73	5.62	6.81	7.31	6.04	4.34
Muslims	5.73	4.50	4.76	5.17	7.29	7.06	4.31	1.85

* Calculated by this author on the basis of the figures in the two preceding statements.

Commenting on the results of this survey, Dr Burman, a Hindu scholar, makes the following highly significant remark:

"If the time when the marriage took place is ignored, the incidence of polygamous marriages in India as a whole is highest among the persons returning their religion as Tribal religions (15.25%), next comes the Buddhists (7.97%) followed by the Jains (6.72%). Among the Hindus 5.8% of the marriages in the sample are polygamous marriages. If all non-Muslims are taken together the result is 5.98%. Among the Muslims it is 5.7%. These data seem to be of considerable interest as they are contrary to the prevailing notion that incidence of polygamous marriages is higher among the Muslims than among other communities. As, however, the marriages were not selected on a random sample basis, it would be risky to draw any quantitative generalisation from these figures. But at the same time it is to be kept in view that the size of the sample is fairly large, and hence until more valid quantitative data are available one would be justified in questioning the validity of the prevailing notion in the matter."

This report does not contain information about the "depth" of polygamy, that is to say, how many wives does every polygamous man have? Dr Burman was himself reported by a newspaper in January 1972 as saying that none of the Muslims had more than four wives whereas the non-Muslims sometimes went as high as fifteen!

Polygamy among the Jews

Polygamy is permitted in Judaism according to Talmudic law.[14] It continued in practice until Rabbi Gershom ben Yehudah (960-1030 AD) convoked a synod and issued an edict against it. The Jewish Sephardic communities living in Muslim countries continued the practice until 1950 when an act of the chief Rabbinate of Israel extended the ban on polygamy to them as well.[15]

The Practice of Polygamy by the Prophet

European writers as well as those Muslim writers who are influenced by European orientalists have created a lot of mischievous propaganda and raised much controversy over the marriages of the Holy Prophet. As we have discussed before, polygamy was an established practice among all the early Biblical and Qur'anic Prophets and extended to the time of the Prophet Muhammad. As a matter of fact, polygamy was never considered undesirable and was an integral part of most social systems throughout the world during the time of the Prophet. The modern problem of the population explosion and the over-exploitation of large tracts of land were not known during that time. Population was sparse and the vast resources of the earth were still lying untapped throughout the world. Naturally there was a burning desire to increase the population. Throughout early history up to the time of the Holy Prophet Muhammad, there was no limit imposed on limitless polygamy. The Prophet was the first person to limit it to four wives on the condition that there was equal justice to all of them.

After the Qur'anic limitation was revealed restricting the system of limitless polygamy, it is a historical fact that the Prophet did not contract any other marriages. We shall discuss what Western writers have failed to understand. The Prophet had only two "normal" marriages, one with Khadijah and the other with 'A'ishah. The other marriages were contracted as a necessity, and that too based on various considerations, by which the Prophet was moved, despite his active life and frugal living, to take another nine wives, demanding a great sacrifice on his part.

It is really surprising that a man living in the *Jahiliyyah* society of the Arabs should spend twenty-five years of his life as a model of chastity and modesty in a social environment where wine and adultery were endemic. It was at the age of twenty-three that he selected a wife who was not a beauty, but a forty year old widow. He spent another twenty-eight years with this single wife, Khadijah. How then can he be accused of sensuousness? The time of his seven and then nine multiple marriages began from the age of fifty-five and extended for four years to the age of fifty-nine.

Among these new wives, all except two were between thirty-six and fifty. His reputation had spread far and wide, not only in Arabia but also in neighbouring countries. Why then could he not get younger and lovelier girls to marry? We have also to consider that the Prophet had taken a marathon task upon himself in building the *Ummah,* the nation of Islam, which did not give him much time for rest or relaxation. The greater part of his time was devoted to affairs of state and society in the nerve centre of Islam, the Masjid an-Nabawi, the mosque in Madina. Even in his hours of privacy he stood in prayer until his feet were swollen. How could such a person be accused of sexual indulgence?

There is absolutely no resemblance between him and other conquerors and rulers given to self-indulgence. He was neither oppressive, nor fond of wine, music or dance, or costly apparel and did not load his consorts with silk and gold and never put their interests above the interests of his mission. Such was the simplicity of the greatest Messenger of Allah. On one occasion when his wives demanded an increase of their meagre allowance, he told them that if they were content with a frugal life they could remain with him, otherwise he would release them with due consideration.

We should also consider here the exclusive and well-defined tribal system of pagan Arabia of those days with its in-built prejudices against men of other clans. In Arabia no-one could carry on the work of reform and upliftment unless he belonged to some specific and respectable clan, and so in the interests of his mission the Prophet needed inter-tribal relationships. He wanted to weld the quarrelling tribal and clannish factions into one Muslim *Ummah* as brethren in faith (*Ikhwan fi'd-Din*). For instance, his wife Juwayriyya belonged to the Banu Mustaliq clan which was very powerful. The entire clan was a bitter enemy of Islam from the start. They were in the forefront of every opposition party and never consented to enter into any pact. At last they were suppressed by military action. But when the Prophet married Juwayriyya, the Muslims released all their prisoners saying that they could not keep the Prophet's relatives in bondage and it was due to this marriage that the whole clan accepted Islam and became peaceful and obedient to the laws of the new Islamic state.

Maymunah also came from a very powerful and recalcitrant clan from Najd and was the sister of the wife of their chief. It was this clan which had brutally murdered seventy members of an Islamic missionary deputation. The Prophet's marriage with Maymunah changed the whole atmosphere and Najd accepted Madinan authority under the leadership of the Prophet. Maymunah's many other sisters were also married to prominent chieftains of the clans and they too now became relatives of the Prophet.

Umm Habibah was the daughter of the Qurayshi chief Abu Sufyan. It was after this marriage that Abu Sufyan never fought against the Prophet. This marriage was largely responsible for the conquest of Makka.

Safiyyah was the daughter of a very prominent Jewish chief, Huyyay ibn Akhtab. In consideration of her family status she could not be merged into an ordinary household. So the Prophet himself married her. After this marriage, the Jews did not dare to revive their opposition to the Prophet and his mission.

In the case of Hafsah, it was the Prophet's desire to bind in relationship those of his great companions *(Sahabah)* who were his advisers and who were trained for future leadership. He had married Abu Bakr's daughter, married two of his own daughters to 'Uthman and one to 'Ali (Fatima). 'Umar could not be kept outside of this circle of relationship. By marrying his daughter Hafsah, the Prophet forged a strong bond of relationship within the Islamic movement, thus strengthening the pillars of the *Ummah*.

The Prophet also contracted a marriage to placate distressed feelings. The Prophet had married his first cousin, Zaynab, to his freed slave, Zayd ibn Haritha, whom he had adopted as his son. It was intended to break family and social barriers but the marriage did not prove a success and ended in divorce. When he saw that Zaynab was left alone, the Prophet felt his responsibility in the matter. He also had to break another convention whereby an adopted son became a real son. This difficult problem was solved by marrying Zaynab (as mentioned in the Qur'an) to annul that pre-Islamic conception and promulgate an Islamic law instead.

The political significance of the Prophet's marriage to Umm Habibah, daughter of Abu Sufyan, has already been mentioned. There is also a further significance. She was first married to a certain 'Ubaydullah and emigrated with him to Abyssinia where 'Ubaydullah became a Christian and a drunkard. Excess of wine killed him. Umm Habibah had held tenaciously to Islam. It was a double shock to her that her husband had become a Christian and died, and she badly needed solace. The Prophet sent 'Amr ibn Umayya al-Zamiri to the Negus of Abyssinia with the proposal of marriage to Umm Habibah, who was so overjoyed that she gave away all her ornaments to her slave-girl. The Negus himself arranged the marriage contract in absentia and paid her a dowry of four hundred gold coins and gave a feast. It is also reported that the marriage was renewed at Madina and another marriage feast was given.

Umm al-Masakin (Mother of the poor and helpless), Zaynab, daughter of Khuzayma ibn Al-Harith, belonged to the Hawazin clan. Her husband gave the supreme sacrifice to the cause of Islam and was killed in the Battle of Uhud. To rescue her from widowhood, the Prophet took her as his wife.

Eleven marriages of the Prophet have been established. Reports of larger numbers are wrong and unconfirmed. Of these, Khadijah died before the Hijra and Zaynab, daughter of Khuzayma, died only three months after her marriage in the third year of Hijra. Thus, in his last days, the Prophet had nine wives with him and out of these, Sawdah, being very old, had given up sexual relations. After restrictions on polygamy were imposed, the Prophet did not marry again. But despite the restriction to four, the Prophet was permitted by revelation to continue all these, for besides the aforesaid considerations, the Prophet's wives were Mothers of the Faithful and if divorced, they would have been left unmarried and unprotected. Furthermore, these wives were engaged in the work of *da'wah* to spread the Islamic way of life among the women. These very women, especially 'A'ishah, became prominent scholars and narrators of the Prophet's *ahadith* and actions, especially in matters pertaining to his family and domestic life. Whenever the early believers needed advice on new problems, they used to call on these *Ummahat al-Mu'minin* (Mothers of the Faithful) and from them they would find the Prophet's answer which they had not known.

If we ponder over the political significance of the Prophet's marital relations, we find that the following clans were thus linked up with the Prophet: (1) Banu Asad ibn 'Abdu'l-'Uzza (2) Banu 'Amir ibn Lu'ayy (3), Banu Taym (4) Banu 'Adi (5) Banu Makhzum (6) Banu Umayyah (7) Banu Asad ibn Khuzayma (8) Banu Mustaliq (9) Arab Jews (10) Banu Kilab, Kalb and Salim, (11) Banu Kindah.

Distributing these clans geographically, we find that the Prophet's position had become inter-tribal which succeeded in uniting all the important clans, ending opposition, restraining ambitions and even suppressing long-standing feuds. For a movement which aimed at establishing universal peace and justice it was beneficial to pave the way by polygamy which was in fact a great sacrifice, which the Holy Prophet undertook for the fulfilment of the noble causes of his Prophetic mission.

Views of Non-Muslims on Polygamy

Dr Annie Besant, an eminent woman scholar, talked about the pretense of monogamy in the Western world in the following words:

"There is pretended monogamy in the west, but there is really polygamy without responsibility. The 'mistress' is cut off when the man is weary of her and sinks gradually to 'the woman of the street' for the first lover has no responsibility for her future and she is a hundred times worse off than the sheltered wife and mother in the polygamous home. When we see the thousands of miserable women, who crowd the streets of Western towns during the night, we must surely feel that it does not lie in Western mouths to reproach Islam for its polygamy. It is better for a woman, more respectable for a woman, to live in Islamic polygamy with respect, than to be reduced to the cast-out on the streets perhaps with an illegitimate child outside the pale of law - unsheltered and uncared for, to become a victim of any passer-by, night after night, rendered incapable of motherhood, despised by all."[16]

Annie Besant further spoke to a British audience in London about polygamy in Islam in the following words;

"You can find others stating that the religion (Islam) is evil, because it sanctions a limited polygamy. But you do hear as a rule this criticism which I spoke about one day in a London hall where I knew that the audience was entirely uninstructed (about Islam). I pointed out to them that monogamy with a blended mass of prostitution was a hypocrisy and more degrading than a limited polygamy. Naturally a statement like that gives offence, but it has to be made, because it must be remembered that the law of Islam in relation to women was until lately, when parts of it have been imitated in England, the most just law, as far as women are concerned, to be found in the world. Dealing with property, dealing with rights of succession and so on, dealing with cases of divorce, it was far beyond the law of the West, in the respect that was paid to the rights of women. Those things are forgotten while people are hypnotised by the words monogamy and polygamy and do not look at what lies behind it in the West - the frightful degradation of women who are thrown into the streets when their first protectors, weary of them, no longer give them, any assistance."[17]

Dr Billy Graham, the world-famous Christian evangelist, says:

"Christianity cannot compromise on the question of polygamy. If present-day Christianity cannot do so, it is to its own detriment. Islam has permitted polygamy as a solution to social ills and has allowed a certain degree of latitude to human nature but only within the strictly defined framework of the law. Christian countries make a great show of monogamy, but actually they practise polygamy. No one is unaware of the part mistresses play in Western society. In this respect Islam is a fundamentally honest religion, and permits a

Muslim to marry a second wife if he must, but strictly forbids all clandestine amatory associations in order to safeguard the moral probity of the community."[18]

Ahmad Galwash has quoted the case of Napoleon Bonaparte who had to divorce his well-loved wife, Josephine, a lady possessing virtues and abilities of a very high order. There was the warmest attachment between the two, but Napoleon could not have issue from her, and the country therefore insisted upon her divorce. The account of her divorce as related by historians and biographers is extremely pathetic. Napoleon married another wife, reigned splendidly and enjoyed the benefits of a prosperous kingdom; then came calamities upon him which continued until his death. Josephine had been divorced, but their love for each other underwent no change. She remembered him with as ardent a love and sympathy in his troubles and calamities as in their days of happiness, but the strong cord which bound them together had been snapped asunder. If polygamy had been allowed, Napoleon and his ex-wife would not have suffered this extreme affliction. Muslim ladies have often allowed their husbands to take another wife in such cases and beget an issue.[19]

If polygamy is not permitted, the result will be sexual anarchy and moral deterioration. In fact, the Western world has deteriorated morally. We can see scholars advocating monogamy. But the unfortunate thing is that they don't think about the other side of the problem. Now some have started thinking boldly on this matter and some western thinkers have come forward to admit the fact that polygamy is a solution for the problem of the number of women far exceeding that of men.

Sir George Scott says that owing to the increase of the female population in this century, those who are for polygamy are not few in number.[20] While discussing this problem, Dr Rom Landau says, "In the light of the evidence collected by History and Science, it is not possible to reject polygamy." [21]

Views of Two Muslim Women Scholars on Polygamy

Islam removed various domestic and conjugal hardships of women by prohibiting the unlimited polygamy prevalent in those days and prevailing nowadays in Western society, though of course in an unacknowledged and unlegalised form.[22]

Maryam Jameelah, an American lady of Jewish extraction who embraced Islam and is a great champion of the cause of Islam, says the following about polygamy in Islam:

"Polygamy is allowed in Islam because all sexual relations outside of marriage are absolutely prohibited. There is no 'double-stan-
dard' recognized by the Shari'ah, as the drastic punishment for the
adulterer and the adulteress are identical. Therefore, if a man cannot
be satisfied with a single wife, if he insists on a relationship with
another woman, he must marry her, undertake her full support and
full paternal responsibility in respect of the children of all his wives.
As a matter of fact, man is polygamous by instinct. Therefore, the
only two alternatives to the limited polygamy permitted in Islam are
divorcing the first wife and throwing her and her children, unprotected and unprovided for, out of the home, or carrying on a secret,
illicit affair with another woman behind the wife's back, deserting
and neglecting her. Of course, no woman wants her husband to take
a permanent rival to herself to share his bed, but the alternatives of
divorce or illicit sex are far worse evils. Some critics will ask, if
Islam allows a man four wives, why is not a woman allowed four
husbands? The reason is that if a man is faithful to his four wives,
the family structure remains intact, but if a woman were allowed to
take more than one husband, family life would be shattered to
pieces because nobody could determine with certainty the real
paternity of the various children. Therefore Islam allows limited
polygamy but prohibits polyandry."23

Sister 'A'isha Lemu, an enlightened English Muslim scholar,
accepted Islam in 1961. She speaks on polygamy from her personal
experience as she is married to a polygamous husband:

"One may observe that, although it has been abused in some
times and some places, polygamy has under certain circumstances a
valuable function. In some situations it would be considered as the
lesser of two evils, and in other situations it may even be a positive-
ly beneficial arrangement.

"The most obvious example of this occurs in times of war when
there are inevitably large numbers of widows and girls whose
fiances and husbands have been killed in the fighting. One has only
to recall the figures of the dead in the First and Second World
Warsto be aware that literally millions of women and girls lost their
husbands and fiances and were left alone without any income or
care or protection for themselves or their children. If it is still maintained that under these circumstances a man may marry only one
wife, what options are left to the millions of other women who have

no hope of getting a husband?

"Their choice, bluntly stated, is between a chaste and childless old maidhood, or becoming somebody's mistress, that is an unofficial second wife with no legal rights for herself or her children. Most women would not welcome either of these since most women have always wanted and still do want the security of a legal husband and family. The compromise therefore is for women under these circumstances to face the fact that if given the alternative, many of them would rather share a husband than have none at all. And there is no doubt that it is easier to share a husband when it is an established and publicly recognised practice than when it is carried on secretly along with attempts to deceive the first wife. And it is no secret that polygamy of a sort is widely carried on in Europe and America. The difference is that while the western man has no legal obligations to his second, third, or fourth mistress and their children, the Muslim husband has complete legal obligations towards his second, third, or fourth wife and their children.

"There may be other circumstances unrelated to war - individual circumstances where marriage to more than one wife may be preferable to other available alternatives, for example where the first wife is chronically sick or disabled. There are, of course, some husbands who can manage this situation, but no-one would deny the potential hazards. A second marriage in some cases could be a solution acceptable to all three parties. Again there are cases in which a wife is unable to have children, while the husband very much wants them. Under western laws a man must either accept his wife's childlessness if he can, or if he cannot, he must find a means of divorce in order to marry again. This could be avoided in some cases if the parties agreed on a second marriage.

"There are other cases where a marriage has not been very successful and the husband loves another woman. This situation is so familiar that it is known as the 'eternal triangle'. Under Western laws the husband cannot marry the second woman without divorcing the first one. But the first wife may not wish to be divorced. She may no longer love her husband, but she may still respect him and wish to stay with him for the security of marriage, for herself and the children. Similarly the second woman may not wish to break up the man's first family. There are certain cases such as this where both women could accept a polygamous marriage rather than face divorce on the one hand or an extra-marital affair on the other.

"I have mentioned some of these examples because to the majority of Westerners polygamy is only thought of in the context of a harem of glamorous young girls, not as a possible solution to some of the problems of Western society itself. I have given some time to it not in order to advocate its indiscriminate use, but in an attempt to show that it is a practice not to be condemned without thinking of its uses and possible benefits in any community."[24]

5

DIVORCE IN THE SHARI'AH

Generally speaking married couples make their best efforts to continue their marital relations in cordiality and happiness. But sometimes relations may go sour and the couple reach the stage where conciliation and counsel have no effect on them and the marriage becomes impossible to continue. The Shari'ah takes a very reasonable view of such an intolerable situation and instead of forcing the couple to stay together in a life of hell (as is the practice in some other systems), permits them to separate in an amicable manner. This method of putting an end to the contract of marriage is called *talaq* (divorce). In order to properly appreciate the position of *talaq* in Islam, it is pertinent to consider the position of divorce in other systems before the advent of Islam.

Divorce before the Advent of Islam

Before the advent of Islam, divorce was practised in different parts of the world in the most inhuman ways. Whenever a man became angry with his wife, whether for valid reasons or just to satisfy his caprice, he could divorce her, but the unfortunate woman could neither have recourse to any legal procedure nor get any maintenance from him nor claim any other kind of right from him.

In Greece, divorce was not guided by any rules or regulations. Even if the couple had vowed to a condition at the time of marriage not to separate from each other, the judge could still grant a divorce if the matter was taken to the court. In the early days of Rome, divorce was an impossibility after the religious rites of marriage had been performed. The husband, however, was given limitless rights over the wife. After quarrelling with his wife, a husband could even murder his wife in order to get rid of her because the religious law did not permit recourse to any legal action for the spouses to separate. However, divorce was introduced among the Romans at a later stage.

The Laws of the Twelve Tables provided for divorce. In addition, a Roman male had the power of summarily putting his wife to death for acts like drinking, poisoning, and substitution of a spurious child. But no Roman wife had the right to sue for divorce and, if she solicited separation, she was liable to punishment for her temerity. As time passed, the facility and frequency of divorce tended to destroy all mutual confidence between spouses and they resorted to divorce even for a trifling dispute. Gibbon says, "In three centuries of prosperity and corruption, the principle of free divorce was enlarged to frequent practice and pernicious abuse. Passion, interest, or caprice suggested daily motives for dissolution of marriage; a word, a sign, a message, a letter, the mandate of freedom, declared the separation; the most tender of human connections was degraded to a transient society of profit or pleasure."

The Methods of Divorce before Islam

Mosaic Law sought to legalise and regulate the husband's power of divorce. But despite the restraints prescribed by Mosaic Law, men enjoyed vast powers to divorce their wives. A man could easily get rid of his wife by levelling a flimsy charge of irreligiosity against her. Even if the husband intended to compromise later on, the matter was beyond his control because after such a charge he was bound by religious code to divorce his wife. Strangely enough, if a woman did not give birth to a child after ten years of marriage, it was essential for the husband to divorce her. Although a husband could divorce his wife for something which made her disagreeable to him, there was no provision for a woman to demand divorce for any reason. Thus there were few or no checks on the arbitrary and capricious use of the husband's power of divorce.

The Christians went a step further than the Jews and declared divorce unlawful. They attributed the rule to the teachings of Jesus, "Whatsoever God has joined together let no man put asunder." (Matthew 5:31-32) They prohibited the man who left his wife from contracting a second marriage. Worse still, they even forbade the unfortunate woman left by her husband from marrying another man.

It was related in Matthew, "It has been said, whosoever shall put away his wife, let him give her a writing of divorce. But I say unto you, that whosoever shall put away his wife, save for the cause of fornication, causeth her to commit adultery; and whosoever shall marry her that is divorced committeth adultery." (Matthew 5:31-32).

Likewise it was said in Mark, "Whosoever shall put away his wife and marry another committeth adultery against her. And if a woman shall put away her husband and be married to another, she committeth adultery." It is surprising that Christianity allowed divorce in the case of adultery of both parties despite its own rule that whatsoever God has joined together, let no man put asunder.

The Roman Catholics so interpret Matthew 5:31-32 as not to provide for divorce at all. They say that since adultery automatically nullifies marriage, there is no need for divorce and, in the case of a wife's adultery, it is not merely lawful but essential for the man to desert her. The Protestants, on the other hand, allowed divorce, but only on grounds of adultery, but considered divorce unlawful on any other grounds - like cruelty, highmindedness or prolonged quarrels. The orthodox Coptic Church of Egypt has made many amendments to the Bible so as to make provision for divorce on grounds of a wife being barren for three years, or her carrying a contagious disease or prolonged quarrels where there is no hope of settlement.

The ancient Hindus considered marriage as an indissoluble tie, enduring even after the death of either spouse. This was the reason why a woman whose husband died in her lifetime had to burn herself alive when the dead body of her husband was cremated.

The pagan Arabs used to divorce their wives at any time, for any reason or even without any reason whatsoever. They also used to revoke the divorce, once given, and then pronounce divorce again and repeat the game as many times as they liked. They also used to swear by one of their idols that they would have no intercourse with their wives, but still continued living with them. They could at their pleasure accuse their wives of adultery, smearing them with such notoriety as would deter other suitors. Even when they dismissed their wives they would go and exempt themselves from any responsibility to give them maintenance and would incur no legal punishment.

Divorce in Islam

In the midst of these different systems which had taken the course of either prohibiting divorce altogether or making it too easy and a plaything, Islam took a middle way. It is recognised that when a marriage becomes impossible to sustain, it is better for the parties to amicably separate rather than being miserably bound together, turning the home into a hell. But, on the other hand, it seeks to make *talaq* a serious buisiness and something abhorrent to Muslims.

Islam's approach to divorce is, indeed, most appropriately viewed in the context of the approach it takes to marriage. Islam recognises marriage as a civil contract and as a contract it should either work or should be revoked if it has ceased to work. Thus it is only in unavoidable circumstances that talaq is permitted in Islam as a lawful method to bring the contract of marriage to an end.

Talaq is a right available mainly to the husband, but not to the wife. Even though Islam allows divorce, the Prophet (peace be upon him) says:

"Of all things that Islam has permitted, divorce is the most hated by Allah." (Abu Da'ud)

This shows that the right is to be exercised only when there are sufficiently compelling reasons to do so. Hasty and wanton use of the right of divorce is regarded as most condemnable in Islam. The Prophet said, "Marry and do not divorce, undoubtedly the Throne of the Beneficent Lord shakes due to divorce."[1]

Thus Islam encourages reconciliation between spouses rather than severance of their relations.

Kinds of Talaq

There are two broad categories of *talaq*:

Talaq ar-Raji' (revocable divorce) which has two forms:

    (i) *Talaq Ahsan* (the most approved divorce)

    (ii) *Talaq Hasan* (approved divorce)

Talaq al-Bain (irrevocable divorce)

This includes *Talaq al-Bida'* (divorce of innovation).

Let us consider the details of these kinds of *talaq*.

Talaq Ar-Raji' (Revocable Divorce)

In this type of divorce the husband pronounces *talaq* once or at the most twice. After the first pronouncement of divorce, the wife's period of *'iddah* starts. Before the end of the *'iddah* is reached, the husband may if he so desires take his wife back. This is called *raja'* or return. But the right of *raja'* will be lost as soon as the *'iddah* is completed and then the *talaq* will cease to be revocable *(raji')* and become irrevocable *(bain)*. The same effect will be produced when the third or last pronouncement is made before the end of the *'iddah*.

It should be clearly noted that the *'iddah* period is only to be observed by a woman whose husband has consummated the marriage. If there is no consummation, there is no *'iddah* and therefore *talaq* is always irrevocable for such a wife however many pronouncements.

Talaq ar-Raji' is based on the following Qur'anic injunction:

A divorce is only permissible twice.
After that the parties should either
hold together on equitable terms
or separate with kindness. (2: 229)

Divorce with the possibily of reconciliation is allowed at the most on only two occasions. After that the parties must definitely make up their minds either to dissolve their marriage permanently or to live honourably together in mutual love and forbearance, neither party worrying the other nor grudging nor evading the duties and responsibilities of marriage. In *Talaq ar-Raji'*, the marital relationship does not disappear till the *talaq* becomes irrevocable. Therefore if one spouse dies during the period of *raja'*, the other will inherit from him or her. *Talaq ar-Raji'* may take one of the two forms: *Ahsan* or *Hasan* which are explained below.

Talaq Ahsan: The term *ahsan* means "the most approved". *Talaq Ahsan* is so named because of the approval it received from the Prophet (peace be upon him).[2] It is in reality intended to prevent a permanent breach between the spouses by providing for the healing factor of time to take its effect and, if possible, soothe the frayed nerves of the parties so that they reunite. The essentials of *Talaq Ahsan* are as follows:

(i) The husband must in the first place pronounce only one *talaq* (i.e. "I divorce you") so that when better sense prevails, he may revoke the *talaq* within the period of *'iddah* for the wife which starts on the pronouncement of divorce.

(ii) The *talaq* must be pronounced only when the wife is in a state of purity after menstruation because during the wife's period the husband may not act on his tender feelings towards the wife on account of the prohibition against sexual intercourse.

(iii) The husband must, after pronouncing the *talaq*, abstain from intercourse with his wife for a period of three months. This period is called *'iddah*.

Considerable light on the wisdom underlying the last two conditions is thrown by a tradition of the Prophet (peace be upon him). 'Abdullah ibn 'Umar divorced his wife while she was having her period. On this being reported to the Prophet, he expressed his exasperation at the levity of 'Abdullah's conduct, "Let him take her back and retain her until she becomes pure and again has her period and again becomes pure. Then if he thinks it prudent, let him divorce her, but he should do so when she is pure and has not been approached; and this is the period of *'iddah* which Allah has ordained for divorce."

Obviously the purpose of the Prophet's admonition was to put a check on the husband taking a rash and hasty course on account of natural aversion against his wife arising from her impurity. By fixing a long period of abstinence to encourage attraction in him towards his wife, the Shari'ah desires the husband to have the opportunity to reconsider his decision about the divorce and for him to exercise the right of return (*raja'*) before the the period of *'iddah* expires.

During *'iddah* the marriage subsists, and the husband retains marital authority over his wife. He may, therefore, have access to the wife even without her permission. If he does so, it would actually amount to exercising the right of *raja'* (return).

The Hanafi jurists are of the opinion that the husband retains the right of reunion right up to the time of the wife's purification by a bath after the third menstrual period. The same opinion was helds by the khalifs, Abu Bakr and 'Ali, and some of the Prophet's other Companions, including 'Abdullah ibn 'Abbas, Abu Musa al-Ash'ari, and 'Abdullah ibn Mas'ud. The Maliki and Shafi'i jurists, however, are of the opinion that the husband forfeits the right of renunion as soon as the wife starts the flow of menstrual blood for the third   period. This opinion was held by 'A'ishah and some other Companions, including 'Abdullah ibn 'Umar and Zaid ibn Thabit. It is the unanimous view of all jurists that the husband retains the right of *raja'*, of reunion, only when he has pronounced one *talaq* or two *talaqs* but he forfeits the right of reunion when he pronounces three *talaqs* in one sitting.

If the husband has pronounced one or two *talaqs* and then he abstains from intercourse with his wife for the entire duration of his wife's *'iddah* period, the divorce becomes irrevocable and he loses his right of *raja'* at the expiration of the *'iddah*. After the divorce, the parties cannot remarry except if there is *tahlil* which is explained below.

Talaq Hasan: The word *hasan* means "approved". *Talaq Hasan* is so named because it commands a degree less in the approval of the Prophet (peace be upon him) as compared to the *Talaq Ahsan*.

In this form, *talaq* is pronounced three times in three successive periods as follows:

(1) The first pronouncement of *talaq* is made in a period of purity from menstruation (*tuhur*) after the husband has decided to divorce his wife.

(2) After the first pronouncement of *talaq* the husband shall not have sexual intercourse with his wife.

(3) A second pronouncement is made in the second *tuhur* followed by sexual abstinence.

(4) If the husband so desires he can repent and reunite with his wife before pronouncing the third *talaq*.

(5) A third pronouncement is made in the third tuhur. When this pronouncement has been made, the divorce becomes irrevocable.

After the divorce has become irrevocable the parties cannot remarry except if there is *tahlil* which is explained below.

Raja' (Right of Return)

The *raja'* or return is the right of the husband. The Qur'an says:

> **And the husband has the better right**
> **to take them back in that period**
> **if they wish for reconciliation. (4: 130)**

It suffices just to utter words like, "I take you back" or the return can be effected through action like resuming sexual relations, kissing each other. According to Imam Shafi'i, the return is not possible without uttering a specific word. According to Imam Malik, it is not permissible to be in privacy with the divorced wife or to have sexual relations with her without her permission, but there is no harm in eating with her.

However, during this period of *'iddah*, the marriage subsists between the parties and the husband retains his marital authority over his wife. He may, therefore, have access to his wife even without her permission. If he does so, it would actually amount to his exercising the right of *raja'* (return).

Talaq Al-Bain (Irrevocable Divorce)

Talaq al-Bain is divorce with three pronouncements of divorce in successive sittings (i.e. *Ahsan or Hasan*) or at the same sitting or divorce before the consummation of marriage. There is no possibility of *raja'* or return to the conjugal relationship when the triple divorce is pronounced and completed, unless the woman has had an intervening marriage.

Talaq Al-Bida'(Divorce of Innovation)

After the death of the Prophet (peace be upon him), a new form of divorce made its appearance as an innovation *(bida')*. In this form, *talaq* becomes irrevocable as soon as it is pronounced. It happens this way: the husband utters the formula, "I divorce you. I divorce you. I divorce you" in one sitting or conveys it to the wife in writing. This form of divorce leaves no room for conciliation and no chance for reconsideration. This is usually done by ignorant Muslims to satisy their selfish motives. When these ignorant people pronounce divorce thrice at the same sitting, they commit a heinous sin against the precepts of the Shari'ah. The Prophet has very severely denounced this practice and the Khalif 'Umar used to whip the husband who pronounced divorce thrice at the same sitting.

Procedure of Divorce in Islam

Islam has introduced many reforms in the procedure of divorce. Divorce may be given either orally or in writing. The Qur'an prescribes that if a man decides to repudiate his wife, he shall call two men of justice (preferably Muslims) to witness his action. (4:129) There is no prescribed formula for pronouncing divorce, but the words used for divorce must expressly convey the intention of the husband that he has dissolved the marriage tie.

For the divorce to be valid it is necessary that the husband should be sane *('aqil)*, not be a minor *(baligh)*, and be capable of using his own discretion *(mukhtar)*.

Therefore a divorce pronounced by an insane person or a child is not considered valid. The Holy Prophet said, "Any divorce is lawful except the divorce given by a person whose intellect is overpowered."

This brings us to the question of whether divorce is valid if given without proper intention (e.g. under the influence of drink or drugs, or in a state of extreme anger, or by way of jest, or just to please somebody) or without free choice (e.g. under threat to his life or property). According to Imam Malik, Imam Shafi'i, Imam Ahmad ibn Hanbal, 'Abdullah ibn 'Abbas and others, such a divorce is invalid. But Imam Abu Hanifah considers it to be valid. Again, all jurists regard the divorce pronounced by mistake as not binding. There is no question of divorce before the solemnisation of marriage.

The triple divorce pronounced at one time, or when the wife is menstruating, or is still bleeding after childbirth, is an innovation, introduced after the days of the Holy Prophet. It is, therefore, called *Talaq al-Bida'*. Such *talaq* is *haram* (unlawful) according to 'Abdullah ibn 'Umar, Sa'id ibn al-Musayyib and Ta'us.[3]

The divorce given to a pregnant woman is binding according to all the madh-habs except the Hanafis.

> **If you fear a break between the two,**
> **then appoint two arbiters,**
> **one from his family and the other from hers;**
> **if they wish for peace,**
> **Allah will cause them to reconcile,**
> **for Allah has full knowledge**
> **and is acquainted with all things. (4:35)**

It is only after the arbitrators fail to effect a rapprochement between the couple that the Qur'an permits them to part company.[4] It says:

> **But if they disagree and must part,**
> **Allah will provide abundance for all**
> **from His all-reaching bounty.**
> **For Allah is He who cares for all and is wise. (4:130)**

If parting becomes necessary, the Qur'an enjoins husbands not to misuse or abuse their power and position and leave the wife in a state of uncertainty, but rather to dispose of the matter one way or the other.

> **You are never able to be fair and just between women,**
> **even if it is your ardent desire;**
> **but turn not away (from your wife) altogether,**
> **so as to leave her (as it were) hanging (in the air).**

**If you come to a friendly understanding,
and practise self-restraint,
Allah is oft-Forgiving, Most Merciful. (4:129)**

On the basis of these Qur'anic injunctions and the traditions of the Prophet (peace be upon him), the jurists of the Sunni schools have classified the circumstances in which divorce may be resorted to in the following situations:[5]

1. Divorce is *wajib* (most essential) in the case of *talaq alhakamain inshiqaq*.

2. Divorce is *makruh* (disapproved) when no harm is anticipated either to the husband or the wife, and there is still some hope of reconciliation between them.

3. It is *mubah* (permitted) when there is need for it, particularly in cases where the wife's character is bad *(su' khulq al-mara'a)* and it is more than likely that harm will arise from the continuance of the marriage.

4. It is *mandub* (recommended) when the wife is not fulfilling the rights which Allah has imposed on her or if she happens to be unchaste.

5. It is *mahzur* (forbidden) when it is given during the days of her monthly period as opposed to the days of *tuhur* (purity) from menstruation.

Mughni al-Muhtaj [6] regards the fifth category of divorce mentioned above as *haram* (unlawful) because it is based on a practice that arose after the time of the Prophet (peace be upon him). It is therefore called the divorce of innovation (*talaq al-bida'*).

Imam an-Nawawi accepts only the categories of *makruh*, *wajib* and *mandub* divorce as mentioned above. All other cases of divorce fall into the *haram* (unlawful) category.

Faskh: Annulment or Abrogation of Marriage

As against the right of *talaq* given to the husband, Islam gives the wife the remedy of *faskh* to bring her contract of marriage to an end. *Faskh* literally means to annul a deed or to rescind a bargain. In relation to marriage, it means the annulment or abrogation of the marital contract by the *Qadi* after the wife has applied to him for this remedy to be granted. If the *Qadi* is satisfied that the woman is prejudiced by her marriage, he will annul the marriage.

The four sunni schools allow the husband the right of *talaq* and the wife the remedy of *faskh* depending on the circumstances necessitating separation between them.

These cases are mentioned below:

Hanafi School
A. Talaq
1. Pronouncement of divorce by the husband.
2. *Ila* (Abstention from sexual intercourse).
3. *Li'an* (Mutual cursing)
4. *Khul'*
5. Separation because of sexual defect *('aib jinsi)* in the husband.
6. Separation due to renunciation of Islam *(Iba)* by the husband.
B. Faskh
In the following cases the *Qadi* or Court may grant the remedy of *faskh* to the wife:
1. Separation due to apostasy of either spouse.
2. Separation due to spoiling of marriage *(fasad)*.
3. Separation due to lack of equality of status *(kafa)* or lack of compatibility of husband.

Shafi'i and Hanbali Schools
A. Talaq
1. Pronouncement of divorce by husband.
2. *Khul'*
3. Declaration of *talaq* by the *Qadi* on the husband's refusal to separate because of *Ila*.
B. Faskh
1. Separation due to defect in either spouse.
2. Separation due to *Li'an*.
3. Separation due to apostasy of either spouse.
4. Separation due to spoiling of marriage *(fasad)*.
5. Separation due to lack of equality of status *(kafa)* of the husband.

Maliki School
A. Talaq
1. Pronouncement of divorce of husband.
2. *Khul'*
3. Separation due to difficulties *(isar)* of the husband in providing maintenance to the wife.
4. Separation due to harm *(darar)*.

5. Separation due to *Ila'*.
6. Separation due to lack of equality of status *(kafa)* or lack of compatibility of husband.
　　B. Faskh
1. Separation due to *Li'an*.
2. Separation due to spoiling of marriage *(fasad)*.
3. Separation due to the renunciation of Islam by either spouse.

Tahlil or Halala

After a divorce has become irrevocable the wife becomes unlawful for the husband in the sense that a prohibition arises that makes immediate remarriage between them unlawful. Since it may sometimes happen that the man repents afterwards and strongly desires to have her as his wife again, a way out of the impasse is provided by the Holy Qur'an:

> **So, if a husband divorces his wife (irrevocably),**
> **he cannot, after that, remarry her**
> **until after she has married another husband**
> **and he has divorced her.**
> **In that case, there is no blame on either of them**
> **if they reunite, provided they feel**
> **that they can keep the limits ordained by Allah.**
> **Such are the limits ordained by Allah,**
> **which he makes plain to those who understand. (2:230)**

Thus the first husband who had irrevocably divorced his wife has permission to re-marry her after she has married a third person and such a person has divorced her. (Of course his death will also have the same effect). This procedure is called *Tahlil* or *Halala*.

Tahlil or *Halala* means legalising or making a thing lawful. In pre-Islamic days, when the wife had been irrevocably divorced by means of pronouncing the triple divorce but the husband wanted to take her back again, the formula was that she married another man on the understanding that he would divorce her without having sexual intercourse with her. No sooner was she divorced by the second husband than she would become *halal* or lawful for the first husband and he would remarry her.

This sort of sham second marriage to get round the prohibition against the husband who had repudiated the first marriage was a trick which in Islam could never be countenanced. Therefore, it is insisted in Islam that the marriage of the divorced woman with the other man should be a genuine marriage containing no condition that he will divorce her. It is also insisted that the second husband must not divorce her without sexual intercourse taking place so that the first husband feels the pinch of jealousy of his former wife lying in bed with a third person due to his own fault in initially divorcing her. But as a matter of law, the divorce by the second husband would become operative even though he had had no sexual intercourse with the woman.

Whatever the legality of the divorce by the second husband, the prohibition against the first husband is the relevant factor. Thus *Halala* was a trick to defeat the prohibition on remarriage between the parties who were separated by irrevocable divorce. This is why the Holy Prophet cursed those who resort to this practice. He said, "The curse of Allah be on the man who commits *halala* and the man for whom the *halala* is committed." The Khalif 'Umar is reported to have said that if they were to bring him two men who took part in the practice of *halala*, he would treat them as adulterers, meaning that the remarriage of the former husband and wife would not be a lawful marriage, but adultery.

Unilateral Divorce on the part of the Husband

After our discussion on divorce, a question may be asked by someone who is not familiar with the Islamic spirit behind this institution. One may ask why the right of divorce is given to a man and not to a woman. When one looks at modern European society as well as those countries where people have adopted Western-oriented legal systems, one finds that both a man and a woman can take either party to court for the dissolution of their marriage. It is then up to the court to declare a divorce.

The Islamic legal system allows a woman to go to a *Qadi* and ask for the dissolution of a marriage on the grounds of cruelty, lack of maintenance, or a husband missing for a long time, or insanity, or in cases where the husband has a dangerous contagious disease such as leprosy, etc. Similarly she can approach a *Qadi* for dissolution of marriage even on grounds of incompatibility as happened in the case of Bint Qais who brought her case to the Prophet saying that she had not seen anything wrong with her husband, but that she had not liked him right from the beginning of the marriage and that she was afraid of being unfaithful in the marriage. The Prophet asked her whether he had given her any dowry at the time of the marriage. She replied that she had been given an orchard which the Prophet asked her to return to him. Then the Prophet persuaded him to divorce her on grounds of incompatibility.

In other words, the right of a woman to dissolve her marriage in the court of the *Qadi* was given to Muslim women 1400 years ago. The Western legal system, which is based on either European or Jewish systems of law, had either made the dissolution of the marriage too loose or too tight. Jewish Law, for example, allowed the husband to write the wife "a bill of divorcement, give it to her hand and send her out of the house" whenever the husband found some uncleanness in her, and the law stated that when "she has departed out of the house, she may go and be another man's wife." (Dt. 24:1,2)

In the case of Christianity, it was too rigid, "What therefore God has joined together let no man put asunder....whosoever shall put away his wife and marries another committeth adultery against her." (Mk. 10: 6,11) St. Paul further said, "Let not the wife depart from her husband." (1 Cor. 7:10) Roman Catholics are of the view that, "When the sacrament of matrimony has been received by man and woman and rectified by their co-habitation as husband and wife, the union cannot be dissolved except by death."[8] In such cases the bond of matrimony becomes a chain as heavy and galling as iron in which two people have to languish for the term of their natural lives.[9] The Protestants only allow for the dissolution of marriage on the grounds of fornication. Islam has steered its course midway between the two, avoiding the extremes of either making divorce too rigid or banning it altogether or making it too loose or frivolous. Islam has thus adopted a middle course in this matter.

As to the question of the right of unilateral divorce granted to the husband in Islam, the following points are worth taking into consideration. A woman's psychological and physiological make-up is such that every month for a period of five to seven days she is in a state of pathological change as discussed by Geddes and Thomson in their book, *Evolution of Sex*.[11] The phenomenon of menstruation in which the blood flows is a normal physiological process of a woman, but her mental energy, as well as muscular strength and dexterity, even in the strongest and healthiest and most determined woman, are usually somewhat impaired during this period.[11] Experts in human biology have also said that there appears to be increased nervous tension and greater muscular excitability during this period; reflex action is more marked and there may be slight twitching of the legs; also yawning and stiffness in the neck, and sleep is usually heavier than usual during this period. In some cases there is loss of appetite and at times there is a certain amount of digestive and intestinal disturbance which amount to a tendency to flatulence.[12]

On the psychological side, even in good health, there is another series of phemonena. There is greater impressionablity, greater suggestibility, and, to a variable extent, diminished self-control. It is also suggested that, at this time, women are more susceptible to hypnosis. It is also during this period that, to those women who are predisposed to them, certain caprices, fits of ill temper, moods of depression, impulses of jealousy, and outbursts of self-confession, are more likely to occur.[13] Also during this period when a woman is exceptionally sensitive and irritable, she may be upset by trivial matters which at other times would provoke no discernible reponse. Likewise the statistics of female criminality shows that a very large majority of crimes committed by women are committed during menstruation.[14]

If women were given the power of unilateral divorce, it is probable that millions of them would divorce their husbands and it is probable that millions of divorces would have ensued and there would be chaos in society. The Qur'an (2: 222) calls menstruation a pollution. It also asks men to keep away from women for the purpose of sexual intercourse until they have purified themselves. This prohibition is more on the ground of hygenic cleanliness and sanitary precautions. It may lead to a series of certain disturbances and in some cases severe monorrhagia, perimetritic irritation and perimetritic inflammations may result as a result of co-habitation.[15]

The Bible stipulates extremely rigid regulations concerning menstruating women: ".....she shall be put apart seven days and whosoever touches her shall be unclean until the even and everything that she lies upon in her separation shall be unclean. Everything that she sitteth upon shall be unclean and whosoever toucheth her shall wash his clothes and bathe himself in water, and be unclean until the even." (Leviticus 15:19-21)

On the basis of the power of unilateral divorce possessed by a Muslim under Islamic law, western scholars have, in their reliance upon deductive logic, jumped to the conclusion that Muslim husbands will be very prone to pronouncing divorce. But the inductively verifiable facts prove quite the contrary. They show that Muslim husbands are very abstemious with their power of divorce. This is understandable because the ethos of Muslim society itself affords a potent check on wanton and reckless exercise of the power of unilateral divorce by Muslim husbands.

Khul': Divorce at the Instigation of the Wife

Khul' is derived from *Khul' al-thawb*, releasing or removing the dress from the body. This has an appropriate allusion to the verse of the Holy Qur'an which says:

Women are your dress and you are their dress. (2:182)

But in its technical sense, it is the name of a method of divorce in which the wife can seek release from marriage.

The Maliki jurists define *khul'* as *al-talaq bil iwad*, or "a divorce by giving something in return."[16] According to the Hanafi jurists, it is the end of a marital relationship with consent either with the utterance of the word *khul'* or something that means the same. The Shafi'i jurists say that "it is a separation sought with something given in return and with pronouncement of the word divorce or *khul'*.[17] It can be achieved through mutual agreement of the two parties or through the order of the *Qadi* on payment by the wife to the husband a certain amount that does not exceed what was given to her as a dowry *(mahr).*[18]

Khul' in the Qur'an and Sunna

The Holy Qur'an permits a wife to ask her husband for a divorce *(khul')* if she fears cruelty or desertion by him. It lays down:

> **If a wife fears cruelty or desertion on her husband's part,**
> **there is no blame on them if they arrange**
> **an amicable settlement between themselves;**
> **and such settlement is best;**
> **even though men's souls are swayed by greed.**
> **But if you practise self-restraint,**
> **Allah is well-acquainted with all that you do. (4:128)**[19]

It is narrated in the Sunnan al-Baihaqi (7:313) that a woman came to the Prophet (peace be upon him) and said, "I hate my husband and want separation from him." The Prophet (peace be upon him) replied, "Would you return the orchard that he gave you as a dower?" She replied, "Yes, even more than that." The Prophet said, "You should not return more than that."

Thus, when the wife feels that her husband is failing to perform the duties imposed on him by the conjugal relationship, she can obtain her release from the tie by giving up all or some of the property received by way of dower (*mahr*) and in consideration of this, the husband may give her a *khul'* which will operate as an irrevocable divorce. But if the wife is not in a position to pay the compensation, there is yet another means to dissolve the marriage by mutual consent. This is called *Mubara'ah* and also operates as irrevocable divorce. However, according to Ibn al-'Arabi, Imam Malik has defined *mubara'ah* to mean *khul'* (release) in consideration of payment before the consummation of marriage, while *khul'* is effected after consummation.[20]

The compensation for *khul'* is a matter of arrangement between the husband and wife through mutual consent. The wife may return the whole or a portion of the dowry received by her. She is not bound to return anything more than the dowry but she may make other arrangements for the benefit of the husband. For instance, she may agree to nurse their child during the two year period of suckling, or to keep and maintain the child at her own expense for a fixed period which is waived at the end of the period of suckling.

The first *khul'* case in Islam is quoted by Imam al-Bukhari (9:329). The wife of Thabit ibn Qais came to the Holy Prophet and said, "O Messenger of Allah, I am not angry with Thabit for his temper or his religion, but I am afraid something may happen to me contrary to Islam on which account I wish to be separated from him." The Prophet said, "Will you give Thabit back the garden which he gave you as your settlement?" She replied, "Yes." Then the Prophet said to Thabit, "Take your garden and divorce her at once."

All the jurists agree on the legality of *khul'*. Imam Malik says that a wife forced by her husband to enter into a *khul'* is entitled to get back the dowry [21], but the separation will be valid under the Shari'ah. The only jurist who does not agree with the legality of *khul'* is Bikr ibn 'Abdullah al-Muzni who seems to fall out of the consensus.[22]

When can Khul' be Demanded?

Khul' must only be demanded in extreme circumstances and not on flimsy grounds. The Holy Prophet has said, "If any woman asks for divorce from her husband without any specific reason, the fragrance of Paradise will be unlawful to her."[23]

Hasan al-Basri has also narrated a *hadith* from Abu Hurairah, "The women asking for separation and *khul'* are hypocrites."[24]

Khul' is disliked *(makruh)* except when there is a fear in the woman that the limits imposed by Allah will not be observed by her if she does not seek release.[25] But according to ad-Dasuqi, *khul'* is not lawful.[26]

Compensation and 'Iddah for Khul'

Once the case goes to court, the *Qadi* must first of all try to ascertain whether the wife really dislikes her husband so much that she cannot live with him any longer. Then, if the court is satisfied that they cannot live together happily, it will fix as compensation anything that it considers proper, and the husband will have to accept this and divorce his wife. The jurists are generally of the opinion that the compensation should not exceed the dowry given by the husband.

As soon as the *khul'* is granted, the husband forfeits the right of reunion after the divorce because it has been brought by the wife. However, it is lawful for them to remarry with mutual consent.

According to the majority of Muslims, the term for *'iddah* for the wife in the case of *khul'* is the same as that in divorce. But Abu Da'ud, Tirmidhi and Ibn Majah and others have related a *hadith* to the effect that the Holy Prophet prescribed only one monthly course as the term for the wife after the divorce, and the Khalif 'Uthman decided a case in accordance with this.[27]

According to the Maliki school, *khul'* is not confined to the utterance of any particular word, some other words like *fidyah, sulh* and *mubarat* can also be used. The word *khul'* is specifically used when a woman asks for a release by returning all that was given to her. *Sulh* refers to part payment. *Fidyah* refers to overpayment and *mubarat* means foregoing the right that the wife has against her husband.[28]

Khul' of a Woman in her Final Illness

According to the Hanafi jurists if a woman seeks *khul'* during her final illness and dies while undergoing '*iddah*, the *khul'* is still valid and the former husband will receive whichever is less out of the following three things:[29]

(1) The amount agreed between the parties as compensation for *khul'*.

(2) One-third of the estate she left after paying her debts.

(3) His share of the inheritance from her.

According to Maliki jurists, *khul'* in a final illness will be valid with all of the one-third (*thulth*).[30] The Shafi'i jurists also regard the*khul'* in the final illness as valid and hold the former husband entitled to receive either the original dowry or one-third of the estate of the deceased, whichever is less. The Hanbali jurists take the same view as the Maliki jurists.[31]

Khul' negotiated by any person (including the father or guardian) other than the wife herself is null and void according to the Dhahiri and Hanbali jurists. But it is valid according to the Hanafi, Maliki and Shafi'i jurists. Al-Muhalla states that *khul'* negotiated by the father is void.[32] Likewise, no one (including the father, guardian, ruler or unrelated person) is allowed to negotiate *khul'* on behalf of an insane or mentally deranged woman or a minor girl. The Shafi'i jurists make no difference between *khul'* negotiated by the father or guardian of a woman or unrelated person.[33] The Hanafi jurists even permit an unrelated person to negotiate *khul'* with the permission of the woman concerned.[34]

The Maliki jurists regard the *khul'* negotiated by a minor girl or an insane woman as unlawful. *Khul'* negotiated by the father on behalf of his minor or insane daughter will, however, be valid whether it is achieved by giving his own property or that of his daughter and whether it is obtained with or without her permission.[35] The Hanafi jurists consider the *khul'* sought by an insane woman or a minor who is not considered responsible (*mumayyazah*) as void.[36]

Can Khul' be Given at any Time?

As a general rule it may be said that the conditions applicable to divorce (*talaq*) also apply to *khul'*. But there are different opinions about the question of whether *khul'* can be given in the period of menstruation. According to *Mukhtasar al-Nafi'*[37] *khul'* should not be given in the period of menstruation. The Ibadis also believe that it is an innovation *(bida')* to give divorce while the woman in menstruating.[38] The Hanafis consider *khul'* during the period of menstruation to be disliked *(makruh)*.[39] But Ibn Abdin says that it is not *makruh* at all[40] since the Holy Prophet did not ask the wife of Thabit ibn Qais about her menstruation when *khul'* was granted by him for her.[41]

Some Maliki jurists say that when the woman is permitted by the Shari'ah to obtain *khul'* in consideration of payment, it is her right to do so even in the period of menstruation.[42] The Hanbali jurists also feel that because *khul'* is brought about by mutual agreement of the parties concerned, menstruation has no effect on its validity.[43]

'Iddah: The Waiting Period

The word *'iddah* is derived from the Arabic word *al-'Adad* meaning the number, in the terminology of the Shari'ah it means a period of waiting from re-marriage after the death of a woman's husband or her separation or divorce from him. Muslim jurists have unanimously agreed on its essentiality *(wajub)*[44] since the injunction of the Qur'an is quite explicit on this subject:

> **Divorced women shall wait by themselves**
> **for three monthly periods. (2:228)**

The Holy Prophet ordered Fatimah bint Qais as follows:
"Complete your *'iddah* period in the house of 'Umar Maktum."

The Shari'ah emphasises reconciliation as a better course than divorce for the married partners and gives them the opportunity to mend their relations if they have gone sour. Therefore, the Holy Qur'an prescribes a period of waiting after divorce has been pronounced so that a spell of temporary separation and suspension of conjugal relations may give the spouses time for rethinking and reconsideration in the interests of family and children, if any, of the question whether divorce should be revoked or made final and irrevocable. The *'iddah* has another very important object to serve, that is, to make it known whether the woman has a child of the former husband in her womb so that there may be no confusion about the paternity of such a child if the woman seeks to remarry.

The Qur'an says:

Divorced women shall wait by themselves
for three monthly periods.
Nor is it lawful for them to conceal
what Allah has created in their wombs,
if they have faith in Allah and the Last Day.
And their husbands have the better right
to take them back in that period,
if they wish for reconciliation.
And women shall have rights
similar to the rights against them,
according to what is equitable
but men have a degree (of advantage) over them.
And Allah is Exalted in Power, Wise. (2:228)

The Different Kinds of 'Iddah

The duration of *'iddah* is prescribed by the Holy Qur'an as follows:

Such of your women as have passed
the age of monthly courses,
for them the prescribed period,
if you have any doubts, is three months,
and for those who have no courses (it is the same).
For those who carry life (within their wombs),
their period is until they deliver their burdens;
and for those who fear Allah,
He will make their path easy. (65:4)

The Qur'an says down that there shall be no *'iddah* for a woman who is divorced by her husband before he has consummated his marriage with her. It says:

O you who believe! When you marry believing women,
and then divorce them before you have touched them,
no period of 'iddah have you to count in respect of them;
so give them a present, and set them free
in a handsome manner. (33:49)

But in casse of termination of marriage due to the death of the husband, widows shall have an *'iddah* of four months and ten days.

The extra period of forty days seems to have been added to provide
for mourning by the widow. The Qur'an says:

If any of you dies and leaves widows behind,
they shall wait by themselves
four months and ten days.
When they have finished their term,
there is no blame on you if they dispose of themselves
in a just and reasonable manner.
And Allah is acquainted with what you do. (2:234)

The different kinds of *'iddah* can be summed up as follows:
(1) *'Iddah* of women who still menstruate: three menstruations.
(2) *'Iddah* of women who have passed the age of menstruation:
three months.
(3) *'Iddah* of a woman whose husband has died: four months and
ten days.
(4) *'Iddah* of a pregnant woman: until she delivers a child.
(5) No *'iddah* for a woman whose marriage has not been consummated.

Some scholars like Ibn 'Abbas have said that since Allah has
made it obligatory for the woman whose husband dies to wait for
four months and ten days, and has the specified period of waiting
for the pregnant woman to last until she has been delivered, it follows that if the husband dies while the woman is pregnant, she is
bound by the two periods concurrently just as she would be bound
to fulfil any other two duties combined together.[45] According to
Imam ash-Shafi'i,[46] the Messenger of Allah said to Subay'ah,
daughter of al-Harith, who gave birth to a child a few days after her
husband's death, "You are lawful (for marriage) and you may get
married." This indicates that the *'iddah,* whether in the case of
death or divorce, was intended to bind women who are not pregnant,
but if they are pregnant the *'iddah* is dropped.[47]

Code of Conduct for Women in 'Iddah

The jurists have different opinions about a woman in *'iddah*
living out of the house. Hanafi jurists say that it is not lawful for a
woman who is given the first and second divorce *(raja')* nor for a
woman who is serving *'iddah* for a *Ba'in* form of *talaq* to go out
of the house either during daytime or at night. But a widow can go

out during the daytime or at certain times at night, but must not spend the night anywhere except in the house. The difference is that in the case of a divorcée, she has the right to be maintained from the property of the husband, and hence it is not allowed for her to leave the house of the husband as a wife. But, in the case of a widow, she is not entitled to maintenance, hence she can go out to seek her provision. According to Hanbali jurists, she can go out during the daytime whether she is in *'iddah* for divorce or as a widow.

Jabir has reported that his aunt was divorced three times, then she went out to cut the fruits of her date-palm. Someone met and told her not to do so. She came to the Prophet and reported the matter to him. The Prophet replied,

"You may go out to cut the fruits of your date-palm so that you may give charity out of it or do something good with it." [Abu Da'ud and an-Nisa'i]

As a precaution, a woman in *'iddah* should not go out at night without any necessity because many evils happen in the dark hours of the night, while during the daytime she can go out to fulfil her necessities and buy whatever she needs. She must not remarry during the period of *'iddah*. *Ahadith* give clear instructions that widows should not wear ornaments and coloured and showy dresses nor adorn themselves with any kind of make-up during this period.

According to Abu Hanifah, she will have the right to her maintenance and a dwelling-place during the period of *'iddah* of irrevocable divorce just as during the *'iddah* of return, but in that case she will have to spend the period of *'iddah* in the matrimonial home. The maintenance will be considered like a debt at the time of the divorce. Imam Malik and Imam Shafi'i say that she will only be entitled to the dwelling-place but not the maintenance except when she is pregnant. Imam Ahmad ibn Hanbal, on the contrary, says that she would have neither right to maintenance nor a dwelling-place.

Treatment of Divorced Women during 'Iddah

The Holy Qur'an prescribes the time when divorce should be pronounced and the treatment that should be given to the divorced woman during *'iddah*. It says:

> **O Prophet, when you do divorce women,**
> **divorce them at their prescribed periods,**
> **and count accurately their prescribed periods;**

and fear Allah your Lord;
and turn them not out of their houses,
nor shall they themselves leave,
except in case they are guilty
of some open lewdness.
Those are the limits set by Allah. (65:1)

Thus when they fulfil their 'iddah
either take them back on equitable terms
or part with them on equitable terms;
and take for witnesses
two persons among you, endued with justice,
and establish the evidence as before Allah. (65:2)

Thus the divorced woman lives in the husband's house until she finishes her *'iddah.* It is not lawful for her to leave it, nor must the husband turn her out of it. Even if she was not present in her matrimonial home at the time of the pronouncement of divorce or separation, it is essential for her to return to the house of her husband. The Qur'an says:

And turn them not out of thier houses,
nor shall they themselves leave
except in cases where they are guilty of lewdness. (65:1)

There is, however, a difference of opinion as to whether a widow should pass the term in the house of the deceased or not. Sayyiduna 'Umar, Sayyiduna 'Uthman, 'Abdallah ibn 'Umar, the four Imams and many other great jurists are of the opinion that she should reside in the house of the deceased husband. Sayyiddah 'A'ishah, Ibn 'Abbas, Sayyiduna 'Ali and some other great jurists are of the opinion that she is free to pass the period wherever she likes.

Remarriage of Widows
In religions like Hindusim and Jainism, re-marriage is not permitted for the widow. Even if the husband dies immediately after her marriage, she has to remain a widow all her life, bearing the taunts of her mother-in-law and sister-in-law. In the first place, she is held responsible for the death of the husband. It is believed that

she brought an ill-omen as a result of which her husband died.

Islam, on the contrary, sympathises with the plight of a widow and encourages her to remarry and start life once again. The Holy Qur'an says:

> **If any of you die and leaves widows behind,**
> **they shall wait by themselves**
> **four months and ten days.**
> **When they have finished their term,**
> **there is no blame on you if they dispose of themselves**
> **in a just and reasonable manner.**
> **And Allah is acquainted with what you do. (2:234)**

Similarly, the Qur'an says:

> **There is no blame on you**
> **if you make an offer of bethothal or hold in your hearts.**
> **Allah knows that you cherish them in your hearts;**
> **but do not make a secret with them except in terms honourable,**
> **nor resolve on the tie of marriage**
> **till the term prescribed is fulfilled**
> **and know that Allah knoweth what is in your hearts,**
> **and tajke heed of Him and know**
> **that God is Oft-Forgiving, Most-Forbearing. (2:235)**

A definite contract of re-marriage for the woman during her period of *'iddah* of widowhood is forbidden as obviously unseemly, as is also any secrecy in such matters. It would bind the women at a time when she is not fitted to exercise her fullest judgment. But circumstances may arise when an offer (open for future consideration but not immediately decided) may be to her interests, and this is permissible.

Nafaqah: The Maintenance of Women and Children

Maintenance (*nafaqah*) is the right of a wife and children to receive food, clothing and a residence and some other essential services and medicine, even if the wife happens to be wealthy in her own right. Maintenance in this form is an obligation (*wajib*) according to the Qur'an, the *Sunnah* and the consensus of the jurists. Where both spouses are above the age of puberty, it is the duty of the husband and not that of the wife, contrary to what happens in some Western countries nowadays, to supply his wife and children with food, clothes and lodging on a scale commensurate with their social position and in accordance with the customs and habits of the society in which they live.

Some jurists made detailed lists of things to be provided as *nafaqah* during the time they were writing about. These must, of course, now be adjusted in the light of modern requirements to suit the circumstances of particular countries and their living standards. It is the responsibility of a father to maintain his daughters until they are married and his sons until they reach the age of puberty. Likewise, it is the duty of every Muslim to maintain his parents and grandparents (maternal as well as paternal) if he can afford to do so. It is even recommended, if a man has the means, for him to look after the needs of his relatives. According to the Hanafi school, every relative within the prohibited degrees is entitled to maintenance if he is a child and poor or if he is an adult but happens to be infirm or blind and poor. In the case that the relative is a female who is poor, she should be maintained whether she is a child or an adult.

If the wife is a minor, she is maintained by her father or guardian. The Messenger of Allah married 'A'ishah two years before she reached the age of puberty and did not give her maintenance. According to Qadi Abu Yusuf, the Hanafi jurist, if the wife is a minor and the husband accepts her in his house, it is essential for him to maintain her, but if she does not come to his house, he does not have to do so.

It is not obligatory for a husband to provide his wife with maintenance in the following circumstances:

(1) If she has packed and moved out of her matrimonial home to some other place without her husband's permission or without any religious cause.

(2) If she has travelled without his permission.

(3) If she has put on *Ihram* for *Hajj* without his permission. However, if she has actually gone on *Hajj* without his permission maintenance should be given.

(4) If she has refused sexual intercourse to her husband.

(5) If she is imprisoned after committing a crime.

(6) If the husband dies and she becomes a widow. In that case her right of inheritance supervenes. This is the reason why a widow is not entitled to maintenance during her *'iddah* period after her husband's death.

According to the Maliki and Shafi'i schools, if a husband fails or neglects to provide maintenance for a period of two years, his wife is entitled to have the marriage dissolved. But in the Hanafi school, inability, refusal or neglect to provide maintenance are not sufficient grounds for dissolution. A wife is entitled to demand from a husband on the point of setting out on a journey either maintenance for the whole duration of his absence, an anticipatory allowance, or that he gives a power of attorney to another to provide for her maintenance. In the latter case the allowance should be paid at the same intervals at which the husband was in a habit of paying it.

Maintenance in the Family

As we have already discussed, it is the husband who is supposed to provide for the family. If he cannot earn enough to support the family, or if his income is too low to provide a relatively acceptable standard of living, and provided the wife is willing, both of them may work for gain. However the following conditions apply:

(1) The husband has the right to terminate the wife's working whenever he deems it necessary.

(2) He has the right to object to any job if he feels that it would expose his wife to harm, seduction or humiliation.

(3) The wife has the right to discontinue working whenever she pleases.

(4) Any gain from work realized by the wife belongs to the family and cannot be considered as her personal property.

When a wife is not employed, the household becomes her first occupation. By household is meant the rearing of children and all domestic services required for maintaining a clean and comfortable habitation. The Prophet says, "Cleanliness is part of faith."

Motherhood is highly recommended in Islam and is of the greatest value second only to to the worship of Allah (*'Ibadah*).

Guidance from the Qur'an and Sunnah on Maintenance

The Holy Qur'an points out the responsibility of maintenance in cases of divorce in the following verse of *Surat at-Talaq* (Divorce):

**Let women in *'iddah* live
in the same style as you live,
according to your means.**

Trouble them not in such a way
as to make things difficult for them.
And if they are pregnant,
then spend your substance on them
until they deliver (the baby):
and if they suckle your child,
give them recompense:
and take mutual counsel together,
according to what is just and reasonable. (65:6)

The husband's responsibility for the maintenance of his wife
and his children by her pertains not only when are living with him,
but continues in the event of divorce. There are some selfish people
who may maltreat their wives and make their lives miserable after
pronouncing the first divorce and while they are still in *'iddah*. This
is forbidden. A wife must be provided for on the same scale as her
husband, according to his station in life. There is still hope of reconciliation, and even if there is not, yet the parting must be honourable.

In the event of pregnancy, the Holy Qur'an imposes additional
responsibility. No separation is possible until after the child is born.
Hence she must be properly maintained. As for the child, its nursing, welfare and similarly the care of the mother remain the father's
duty. If the mother's milk fails, or if circumstances arise which bar
the natural course of the mother's nursing her child, it is the father's
responsibility to give the child to someone else to suckle at his own
expense. Thiscontingency, however, must not induce the father to
cut down the reasonable maintenance to which the mother is entitled.

The Holy Qur'an gives further guidance regarding the matter of
maintenance in *Surat al-Baqara*:

Mothers shall give suck to their offspring
for two whole years,
if the father wishes to complete the term.
But he shall bear the cost of their food and clothing
on equitable terms. (2:233)

In the above injunction, the word *rizq* is mentioned which
includes sufficient food, adequate clothing and other necessary pro-

visions.

The verse specifically mentions the maintenance of the child so that no selfish people on either side may use the child as an excuse for driving a hard bargain, whether from the mother or the father.

> **No mother shall be treated unfairly**
> **on account of her child**
> **nor father on account of his child,**
> **and they shall be chargeable**
> **in the same way. (2:233)**

The father and mother must conclude all the arrangements for the maintenance of the child by mutual consent. They must agree to some course which is both reasonable and equitable regarding the period before weaning, the maximum time of which is two years, even if a wet-nurse is engaged or if the child is fed on artificial milk and feed. Further guidance on the subject is offered in the following verse:

> **Let the man of means spend according to his means,**
> **and the man whose resources are restricted,**
> **let him spend according to what Allah has given him.**
> **Allah puts no burden on any person**
> **beyond what He has given him.**
> **After difficulty, Allah will soon grant him relief. (65:7)**

As befits a practical religion, the *Shari'ah* of Islam does not impose undue burden on either party. They must do their best in the interest of the child according to their means. If they act with honest integrity, Allah will provide a solution to their problem.

The necessity of providing maintenance is emphasised in the address the Prophet made during the Farewell Pilgrimage, the *Hajj al-Wida'*:

"Beware of your treatment of women. You have accected them with the word of Allah...and you have a duty to provide them with reasonable maintenance and clothing."

In a *hadith* narrated by 'A'ishah, Hind bint 'Utbah once said to the Prophet, "O Messenger of Allah, Abu Sufyan is a miserly person. He does not provide for me and my son except whatever I take away myself secretly about which he does not know." The Prophet advised, "Take whatever is sufficient for you and your son in a reasonable way."

According to Maliki jurists, it is the duty of the husband to provide accommodation for his divorced wife if he has consummated the marriage. No maintenance is due to a divorced woman, however, except where the divorce is less than three pronouncements. But a pregnant woman, whether repudiated once or thrice, is entitled to maintenance. A woman who has separated from her husband under the system known as *khul'* is not entitled to maintenance except when she happens to be pregnant. But any woman who becomes separated from her husband through *li'an* (mutual cursing) cannot claim maintenance from that husband, even if she happens to be pregnant.

According to the Maliki school, a wife observing her *'iddah* due to the death of her husband is not entitled to maintenance. But she is entitled to accommodation if the house she happens to be staying in belonged to her husband or if the deceased had paid rent in advance. Imam Abu Hanifa says that she is entitled to her maintenance as well. A wife must not leave her house, either in the case of of divorce or the death of her husband, until she has completed the *'iddah* prescribed for the occasion.

In the Hanafi school of law, as laid down in *Durr al-Mukhtar*, the wife will be treated as *asl* (root) and the child as *far'* (branch) in establishing priority in awarding maintenance, although both are inseparable and their maintenance is *wajib* according to the jurists of all schools.

The wife is not entitled to past maintenance except under the Shafi'i school. The Shi'ites agree with the Shafi'is in this regard.

In fixing the sum to be paid for maintenance, all the schools lay down the rule that the *Qadi* in exercising his discretion should consider the rank and circumstances of both the spouses. But the following conditions must be fulfilled:

(1) It must be a valid marriage.
(2) The wife must submit herself to her husband and be obedient to him.
(3) The wife must give him free access at all times.
(4) The wife must not refuse to accompany her husband when he travels unless she strongly feels that during the journey her person and her property will not be safe.

If the above conditions are not fulfilled a wife is not entitled to maintenance. The husband's duty to maintain his wife commences when she attains puberty and not before.

Rada': Suckling

In order to ensure that children are properly fed, clothed and looked after, the Holy Qur'an lays down rules in respect of *rada'* (suckling). These rules are meant to safeguard the interests of children both when the marriage between the parents continues and when the marriage ends in divorce. If the marriage between the parents continues, it is the responsibility of both of them to look after their child and not neglect it, since it is incapable of taking care of itself. If their marriage ends in divorce, they should agree to some reasonable and equitable arrangement for the care of their child. *Rada'* or suckling is a duty incumbent on both parents and if they neglect it, they will be answerable to Allah on the Day of Judgement. The maximum period of suckling is two years. If the father of the child is afraid that the mother will neglect the child, he should engage a wet-nurse. In modern times this will include arrangements for bottle feeding. The injunction of the Qur'an goes on:

> **Mothers shall give suck to their offspring**
> **for two whole years,**
> **if the father wishes to complete the term,**
> **but he shall bear the cost of their food and clothing**
> **on equitable terms.**
> **No soul shall have a burden laid on it**
> **greater than it can bear.**
> **No mother shall be treated unfairly**
> **on account of her child,**
> **nor father on account of his child,**
> **and they shall be chargeable in the same way.**
> **If they both decide on weaning by mutual consent,**
> **and after due consultation,**
> **there is no blame on them.**
> **If you decide on a foster-mother for your offspring, there is no**
> **blame on you,**
> **provided you pay (the mother) what you offered,**
> **on equitable terms.**
> **But fear Allah and know**

that Allah sees well what you do. (2:233)

The points which become clear from the above verse of the Holy Qur'an are as follows:

(1)The period of giving suck is normally two years.

(2) The responsibility for providing maintenance to the wife or former wife and for arranging such for the child is on the man. He shall bear the cost of food and clothing on equitable terms.

(3) The woman who gives suck to her baby should not be maltreated by her husband.

(4) The weaning of the child should be done by mutual agreement between the mother and the father.

(5) If the man dies, his heirs will be responsible for maintenance of his widow and the suckling of his child.

(6) If, by any chance, the mother herself cannot give suck and she and her husband decide to employ a foster-mother, there is no harm. But the mother should still be given her maintenance.

(7) Every Muslim should know that whatever he does, Allah sees him all the time, therefore he should not treat his wife or former wife and his child unfairly.

Period of Suckling

A child should be suckled for a period of two years at the end of which it should be weaned. However, the period may be extended if there are special circumstances to warrant it. The Holy Qur'an says:

> **And we have enjoined on man**
> **(to be good) to his parents.**
> **In travail upon travail**
> **did his mother bear him,**
> **and his weaning is in two years:**
> **show gratitude to Me and to thy parents;**
> **to Me is thy final goal.(31:14)**

It says further:

> **The carrying of the child to his weaning**
> **is a period of thirty months. (46:15)**

Commenting on this verse, 'Allamah Yusuf 'Ali says:

"It leaves six months as the minimum period of human gestation after which the child is known to be viable. This is in accordance with the latest ascertained scientific facts. The average period is 280 days, or ten times the inter-menstrual period, and of course the average period of weaning is much less than 24 months."

Orphans and their Guardianship

The person and property of orphans is generally exposed to many risks. Therefore Islam gives special attention to the protection of the interests of orphans by their guardians. The Qur'an says:

> They ask thee concerning orphans.
> Say: The Best thing to do
> is what is for their good.
> If you mix their affairs with yours,
> they are your brethren;
> but Allah knows the man who means mischief
> from the man who is put into difficulties.
> He is indeed Exalted in Power, Wise. (2:220)

> To orphans restore their property
> (when they reach their age),
> nor substitute (your) worthless things
> for (their) own good ones:
> and eat not their substance
> (by mixing it up) with your own,
> for this is indeed a great sin. (4:2)

> To those of weak understanding (orphans and others) make not
> over your property,
> which Allah has made means of support for you,
> but feed and cloth them therewith, and speak to them words of
> kindness and justice. (4:5)

> Make trial of orphans
> until they reach the age of marriage;
> if then you find sound judgement in them,
> release their property to them;
> but consume it not wastefully,

nor in haste against their growing up. (4:6)

The words "your property" are used in respect of an orphan's property in the Qur'an with the meaning that all property belongs to Allah and anyone who possesses it or administers it is merely a custodian. Ultimately all property belongs to the community and is for their good. It is only held in trust by individuals. Guardians are advised as to how to administer the property of orphans. If the guardian is well off, let him claim no renumeration, but if he is poor, let him have for himself what is just and reasonable. When you release their property to them, take witnesses in their presence but Allah is all sufficient in taking account.

These verses are very comprehensive in meaning. They teach the Muslim community that in no case should wealth, which is so important for the maintenance of life, be entrusted to people who are feeble-minded and incapable of using or managing it properly, for they might, by its wrong use, spoil a society's cultural and economic system and in the long run its moral system as well. It is true that the rights of private ownership must be honoured, but at the same time they are not to be so unlimited as to allow someone to use them in any way they like and so create social chaos.

As far as the necessities of life are concerned, they must be taken care of, but none should be allowed to use these rights to the extent that they become harmful to the collective moral, cultural and economic good of the community.

Every owner of wealth should consider seriously before entrusting their wealth to anyone, whether that person is capable of using it properly. On the larger scale, the Islamic State should take into its own custody the property of those who are found incapable of using it properly, or of those who may be using it in wrong ways but should, of course, arrange for provision of their necessities of life. The Qur'anic statement, "Make trial of orphans until they reach the age of marriage", gives guardians an additional responsibility to keep an eye upon them and to go on testing their intelligence to see how far they have become capable of looking after their own affairs before giving them back their property.

In other words two conditions, puberty and sound judgment, have been laid down for the return of orphans' property to them. As to the application of the first condition, all the jurists are agreed about it, but as regards the second condition there is some difference of opinion. Imam Abu Hanifah is of the opinion that if the orphan lacks capability when he reaches the age of puberty, his guardian may wait for a maximum period of seven years, and then he must return his property to him whether he shows signs of capability or not. But Imam Abu Yusuf and Imam Muhammad and Imam Shafi'i are of the opinion that capability is a pre-requisite for the return of an orphan's property to him. Probably these latter learned people were inclined to the opinion that the case of such a person should be referred to a Muslim *Qadi*, who would himself arrange for the management of the property of someone who was not capable of managing it himself.

Guardians are further advised:

> **But if at the time of division,**
> **other relatives or orphans or poor are present,**
> **feed them out of the property**
> **(although they have no legal share)**
> **and speak to them**
> **words of kindness and justice. (4:8)**

> **Those who unjustly eat up the property of orphans,**
> **eat up fire into their own bodies:**
> **they will soon be enduring a blazing fire. (4:10)**

The cause of revelation of this verse is mentioned in the books of *ahadith*. When Sa'd ibn Rabi'ah, a Companion of the Prophet, was killed in the Battle of Uhud, his widow came to the Prophet with his two daughters and said, "O Messenger of Allah, these are the two daughters of Sa'd, the one who was martyred in the Battle of Uhud. Their uncle has taken away all the property belonging to Sa'd and has left nothing for the children. Who will marry these girls? It was then that this verse was revealed to give warning to those who consume the property of orphans.

The Qur'an urges people to be fair and just to orphans, especially when they want to marry female orphans. It says:

> **They ask thy instruction concerning the women,**
> **say Allah does instruct you about them:**
> **and (remember) what has been rehearsed unto you**
> **(to be just in your dealings**

with women, orphans and children
and those who really require special consideration)
in the Book, concerning the orphans of women
to whom you give not the portions prescribed,
and yet whom you desire to marry,
as also concerning the children
who are weak and oppressed:
that you stand firm for justice to orphans.
There is not a good deed which you do,
but Allah is well-acquainted therewith. (4:127)

It also says:

If you fear that you will not be able
to deal justly with the orphans...(4:3)

The cause of revelation of this verse was that there was, under the care of a man, an orphan girl who owned a date-palm. He married her just because she owned the date-palm and not because he loved her. It was on that occasion that this verse was revealed.

6

ZINA (ILLICIT SEXUAL INTERCOURSE)

Zina and its Severe Punishment

Zina means sexual intercourse between a man and a woman not married to each other. It is immaterial whether it is adultery (where the participants are married people) or fornication (when they are unmarried). Islam regards *zina* in any case as a great sin:

> **Do not come near to adultery**
> **for it is a shameful deed and an evil,**
> **opening the road (to other evils). (17:32)**

The Prophet, upon him be blessings and peace, declared *zina* to be the greatest evil after *shirk* (association of something with Allah). He said:

"There is no sin after *shirk* greater in the eyes of Allah than a drop of semen which a man places in the womb which is not lawful for him." (Al-Bukhari, *Kitab al-Hudud*)

Of course, Allah has reserved great torments for adulterers in the Hereafter. The Prophet is reported as saying that a most foul smell would emanate in Hell from the private parts of an adulterer. He is also reported to have said that Allah will open in the grave of the adulterer eighty doors of hell from which will emerge scorpions and snakes to bite him until the Day of Resurrection.

Islam abhors adultery and enjoins upon Muslims to keep away from all those things which might prove to be steps leading towards it. Since a passionate look at an unknown woman is the the first such step, it is prohibited by the Prophet in the following words:

"Even to look at an unknown woman (with a passionate eye) is also a sin."

Other steps towards adultery are prohibited by the Prophet in the following words:

"The adultery of legs is walking (with bad intention towards a woman who is not lawful for a man) and the adultery of the hands is touching and patting (such a woman) and the adultery of the eyes is casting passionate glances at her."

Punishment for Zina
There are definite *hadd* punishments for adulterers mentioned in the Qur'an and the *Sunnah*. The Qur'anic injunctions were revealed little by little so as to be easily acceptable to the new converts to Islam who were steeped in the vice of *zina* during the Days of Ignorance. The first revelation was about women. It said:

> **If any of your women are guilty of adultery,**
> **take the evidence of four (reliable) witnesses**
> **from amongst you against them,**
> **and if they testify confine them to houses**
> **until death do claim them,**
> **or Allah ordains for them some (other) way. (4:15)**

The second revelation covered both men and women:

> **If two persons among you are guilty of adultery,**
> **punish them both.**
> **If they repent and amend themselves,**
> **leave them alone,**
> **for Allah is Oft-returning, Most Merciful. (4:16)**

The third revelation prescribed a specific punishment for adultery. It reads:

> **The woman and the man guilty of *zina*,**
> **flog each of them with a hundred stripes;**
> **let not compassion move you in their case,**
> **in a matter prescribed by Allah,**
> **if you believe in Allah and the Last Day;**
> **and let a party of the believers**
> **witness their punishment. (24:2)**

When this verse was revealed, it was understood that those guilty of adultery should be given a hundred lashes as a punishment. The Prophet, may Allah bless him and grant him peace, clarified the injunction:
"Take from me, accept from me. Undoubtedly Allah has now

shown the path for them. For unmarried persons, the punishment is one hundred lashes and exile for one year. For married adulterers, it is one hundred lashes and stoning to death." (Al-Bukhari, *Kitab al-Hudud*)

Some jurists take the view that because a person guilty of adultery is to be stoned to death, there is no need to punish him with a hundred lashes. They take support from the fact that the Prophet stoned two Jewish adulterers to death and did not punish them with lashes. But Khalif 'Ali punished a woman with lashes on a Thursday and stoned her on a Friday. He maintained that he gave the lashes in accordance with the command of Allah and stoned her according to the command of the Messenger of Allah.

The following conditions must first be fulfilled before a person can be stoned to death as a punishment:

(1) The offender must be sane.
(2) He must be a Muslim.
(3) He must be married.
(4) He must have reached the age of puberty.

The Method of Punishment

The idea behind awarding such a severe punishment for adultery in an open place is that it should serve as a deterrent to other evil-minded persons in society. A very heavy responsibility lies on the *Qadi* (the judge) in sentencing a person to be stoned to death. He must fully satisfy himself that there is the unshakeable testimony of four reliable and pious Muslim witnesses that they saw the accused persons actually committing the offence. If there is the slightest doubt in the testimony of the witnesses, its benefit must go to the accused who should be acquitted. Another method of proof of the accused's guilt is when such an accused person voluntarily makes the confession of his or her guilt in one sitting. If the accused confesses three times but retracts the confession the fourth time, he or she should not be stoned to death.

It is narrated by Jabir ibn 'Abdullah al-Ansari that a man from the tribe of the Banu Aslam came to the Holy Prophet and told him that he had committed adultery. He bore witness four times against himself. The Holy Prophet ordered him to be stoned to death as he was a married man. (Al-Bukhari, *Kitab al-Hudud*)

Many scholars feel that because the Holy Qur'an does not specifically mention the punishment for adultery to be stoning to

death, it is not justifiable to stone an adulterer to death. This is
precisely what the Khalif 'Umar tried to forestall. Ibn 'Abbas has
reported:
     'Umar said, "I am afraid that after a long time has passed,
people may say, 'We do not find the verses of *rajm* (stoning to
death) in the Book of Allah,' and consequently they may go astray
by leaving an obligation that Allah has revealed. Lo! I confirm that
the penalty of *rajm* be inflicted on him who commits illegal sexual
intercourse if he is already married and the crime is proven against
him."

The Permissive Society and Unmarried Mothers

     Recently, startling statistics of unmarried mothers, both among
blacks and whites, have been released. It gives the impression that
slowly and gradually even the stigma of becoming an unwed mother
has almost disappeared. Young girls, some of them 15 years old, do
not go for abortion, but are proud of having their babies. *Time
Magazine* of November 9, 1981, published the following report:
"According to federal figures, illegitimate births increased so
rapidly in the 1970's that 17% of U.S. babies - one out of every six -
are now born out of wedlock. In 1979, the last year for which
statistics are available, an estimated 597,000 illegitimate babies
were born to white teenagers and 83% of the babies born to black
teens were illegitimate."

     The report further says that the black community accounts for
more than half of the illegitimate births, but the overall black
illegitimacy rate has, in fact, dropped fairly sharply over the decade.
It was down by 10.7%, from 95.5 births per thousand unmarried
women in 1970 to 85.3 in 1979, while the white rate rose by 8.6%,
from 13.9 per thousand to 15.1 per thousand. The number of
abortions has also increased dramatically, but still "...among
unmarried teens there are three live births for every abortion. Today
about 1.3 million children live with teenage mothers, about half of
whom are unmarried."

     The reason for so many women giving birth out of wedlock is
because the social stigma against being an unmarried mother has
declined. Girls are no longer thrown out of most high schools for
getting pregnant, or packed off to a home for unwed mothers. In the
late '60s and early '70s, the report says, about 71% of unmarried
white pregnant teenagers and 26% of blacks married in haste before

the birth of a child. By the late '70s, the number had fallen to 58% of whites and only 8% of blacks. Major Helen Warnock, director of a Salvation Army maternity home outside Tulsa, says, "Just a short time ago, getting pregnant when you weren't married was the worst mistake a 'nice' girl could make. Now, having a baby is a kind of status symbol."

The other reason for illegitimacy is more sex among younger people in the pleasure-oriented society of the West. Says Jane Murray of the Alan Guttmacher Institute, which specializes in family planning, "We live in a world of tight jeans." Captain Carl Bryant, who runs the Salvation Army's Booth Memorial Home for Unwed Mothers in Chicago, talked of the paradoxical sophistication of the 13 or 14 year-old girl who tries to "act older, just like Brooke Shields, but does not connect intercourse with pregnancy in any meaningful way."

A recent study done at Johns Hopkins University showed that only 14% of teenagers seek birth control advice before their first sexual encounter. For some girls, having an illegitimate baby is a sought-after sign of maturity. Says James Whitten, director of Harlem's Reality House, "They would prefer marriage, but if it doesn't happen, O.K., they want to show they accept responsibility." Others simply want a cuddly plaything. One pregnant 14 year-old said of course she knew how to care for her baby, "I'm going to dress it up real warm in little clothes, stuff like that. You know, be a mother." Says Jeanette Alejandro of Brooklyn, who dropped out of school after eighth grade to have a baby out of wedlock: "I guess everybody wants a baby. Probably to fill in their life. They feel so bored. They got nothing to do with this life."

During the '70s, the rate of unwed births in American ran well ahead of the increase in the number of women of child-bearing age. The most recent statistics are among the worst: illegitimate births for 1979 were up almost 10% over 1978. The cost to tax-payers for illegitimate child-rearing has gone very high, and in 1981, "the federal program for Aid to Families with Dependent Children is expected to exceed seven billion."

Punishment for Adultery in the Shari'ah

At the conference on Muslim Doctrine and Human Rights in held in, Riyadh, March 23, 1972), between Saudi Arabian scholars and European jurists, the Muslim *'ulama'* gave the following arguments in favour of the *hadd* punishment for adultery, "This penalty is prescribed only when the culprit, prior to his delict, had contracted a legal marriage, and if four witnesses known for their righteousness and their integrity, were present at the accomplishment of the sexual act, in a manner which would exclude the possibility of any doubt; it would not be sufficient that they had seen the accused completely naked and stuck together."

The Delegation went on to say: "Here again, we agree with our guests on the severity of the punishment. Nevertheless, it is not imposed in Islam unless the fact, as we just said, was testified to by four objective and trustworthy witnesses. The testimony of one witness has no value before the law; in that case, the person is advised to refrain from making the denunciation, and condemned to be scourged, if he would continue in his accusation; the same thing happens, if there are only two, or even three witnesses. The primary condition, required by the verse, is the presence, at the moment of the act, of four witnesses who can be trusted, and have never been indicated. But if the act was accomplished in the presence of four witnesses, the judgement is that public order has been seriously offended. Whether legitimate or not, it is always improper for the sexual act to take place in public. That is why Islam reveals the most severe attitude against offenders of public order and morality. We suppose that, if such a thing occurred in the street of the capital of a civilized country, where complete sexual liberty is allowed, passers-by would have taken upon themselves to lynch the performers, even before the case could be laid before a court. Such people would be treated like beasts, and their lives would not deserve any more respect."

Then, the Delegation proceeded: "It must be noted, in this matter, that the hard punishment of adultery was prescribed at the very beginning of the Islamic message. There was, at that time, an urgent necessity to bring society out of a system, where existed, in numerous walks, absolute sexual licence, and by the very fact there was utter confusion with regard to paternity, into a new order, where procreative instinct was regulated, and could be exercised only within the limits of legitimacy. And so, from the beginning of the Islamic predication, and during the whole life of the Prophet, not one single case of adultery was established by the evidence of four eye-witnesses. Only one case was verified, through the spontaneous confession of the culprit eager to purify himself in this life, and so escape the punishment in the other. When, coming to the Prophet, he confessed his crime, and asked to be stoned to death, the Prophet turned his face and refused to listen. Since the act had been accomplished in secret, and thus public order and morality did not suffer, the matter concerned only the culprit, who, in his soul and conscience, had simply to beg the Lord's forgiveness. The man, however, earnestly renewed his confession and his request, so as to prove his sincerity towards God, and to deter others from committing the same crime; again, the Prophet turned his face. The same happened a third time, but when the culprit repeated his words a fourth time, the Prophet asked him if he had become insane, or had really admitted being guilty of the crime. First by refusing to listen, then by questioning the fact, the Prophet had long prompted him to retract, but the man so insisted, that in the end his demand had to be heard. At the moment of the execution, however, he regretted his declaration and ran away, the punishment squad ran after him and killed him. The Prophet then pronounced his famous sentence, 'Would that you had left him alive; he would have repented and God would have been merciful to him.' "

The Delegation continued: "Thus gentlemen, it was not possible to prove, by such evidence as is required, one single case of adultery at the time of the Prophet; and yet, it was an age of transition from general sexual licence to discipline and legality on this point. Fourteen centuries have elapsed since that most severe penalty was edicted, and we can strongly affirm that fourteen cases of stoning could hardly be remembered in all that time. In this way, punishment by stoning has remained what it always was, cruel in principle, but extremely rare in practice. But, through the very ruthlessness of this provision, Islam has prevented dislocation of the family and confusion with respect to paternity. We surely admit that men are always men, but it remains that, under a secular legislation, where such a severe punishment, religiously motivated, is lacking, married people end up losing the fear of God, and are more tempted to fall in this crime. Generally speaking, the state of things prevailing in non-Muslim countries has caused the dissolution of family ties, and jeopardized the conjugal happiness, which Muslim husbands and wives, faithful to one another, to their religion, and to God, enjoy."

Commenting on the subject, His Excellency Doctor Dawalibi made the following observations. These were addressed in particular to the President of the European Commission, who had, before leaving for Saudi Arabia, heard from some people hostile to Islam the remark, "So you are going to the country where they lynch women for adultery?"

"If you please, Mr President, report to these people what you have heard. You have neither heard that anyone has been stoned, nor seen any such thing in this Kingdom. It is better in a society where the fear of God is enough to prevent both crime and punishment, thus securing integrity of the family and happiness of the married couple, to prescribe a strict religious penalty in this matter, rather than rely on a secular legislation which does not provide any similar penalty, but does not instil in man any fear of God either, and which, by the same token, causes many to lose the sense of the family. There inevitably follow offences to social dignity, and encouragement to crimes of the most dreadful and varied kinds, whereas, in Muslim countries, where God is openly revered, and His Law sincerely enforced, nothing comparable happens."

Punishment for Qadhf (Defamation of Innocent Women)

Qadhf or defamation is an offence which comes into existence when a person falsely accuses a Muslim of fornication or doubts his paternity. It is a great crime in Islam and those who commit it are called wicked transgressors by the Holy Qur'an which reads:

> **And those who launch charges against chaste women,**
> **and do not produce four witnesses**
> **(to support their allegation),**
> **flog them with eighty stripes.**
> **And reject their evidence ever after.**
> **For such men are wicked transgressors. (24:4)**

Every Muslim is supposed to guard the honour and respect of all Muslim women and not expose the hidden failings of any other Muslim. If a person accuses a Muslim of adultery and cannot prove it by producing four witnesses who have seen the act being committed at the same time and in the same place, the accuser will be punished with eighty lashes. He will be considered *fasiq* and as such his evidence will no longer be accepted whenever he comes forth to give it.

It is reported by Abu Hurayrah that the Prophet, upon him be blessings and peace, said, "Keep away from seven abominable acts." He was asked, "O Messenger of Allah, what are they?" The Prophet replied, "Association of partners with Allah, magic, killing someone, which is forbidden by Allah except when it is with the injunction, consuming usury, devouring the property of orphans, turning away from the day of *jihad* in the path of Allah and *the slander of chaste but indiscret women.*" (Al-Bukhari)

'Ubada ibn as-Samit, who took an oath of fealty to the Prophet with a group of people reports that the Prophet included a prohibition against defamation:

"I take your pledge that you will not worship anything besides Allah, will not steal, will not commit infanticide, *will not slander by forging false statements and spreading it,* and will not disobey me in anything good. And whoever among you fulfills all these, his reward is with Allah. And whosoever commits any of the above crimes and receives his legal punishment in this world, that will be his legal expiation and purification. But if Allah screens his sins, it is up to Allah who will either punish of forgive him according to His wish."

At times good and chaste women tend to be simple-hearted and indiscreet (*al-ghafilat*). This may lead them into some problems through the evil manoeuvres of some selfish and jealous people. Such was the case of the Mother of the Faithful, 'A'ishah as-Siddiqa. A slanderous charge was spread about her which put not only her, but also her husband, the Prophet himself, and her father Abu Bakr, in a most painful predicament. It might have had the most serious repercussions on the *ummah* in its formative years and affected the great work which the Prophet was engaged at that time. But, fortunately, Allah exposed the falsehood of the accusation through revelation.

In this connection, the Qur'an says:

> **Those who slander chaste women,**
> **indiscreet but believing,**
> **are cursed in this life and in the Hereafter;**
> **for them is a grievous penalty;**
> **on the day when their tongues,**
> **their hands and their feet**
> **will bear witness against them**
> **as to their actions. (24:23-24)**

According to Imam Malik and Ahmad ibn Hanbal, even if a person accuses someone merely by implication, it is sufficient to punish him with eighty lashes. But according to Imam Abu Hanifah and Imam Shafi'i, the accused should be asked about his intention in making the accusation before punishment is rewarded to him. If he says that he did not mean to slander the woman, then he shall be punished only by *ta'zir* (discretionary punishment).

Repentance of the Slanderer
The Holy Qur'an says:

**Unless they repent and mend their behaviour,
then Allah is Oft-forgiving, Most Merciful. (24:5)**

Therefore if the slanderer, after receiving the punishment of eighty lashes, repents and gives an assurance that he will not engage in a similar activity in the future, his civic rights of giving evidence are restored. But Imam Abu Hanifah takes a different view and considers that neither the punishment of eighty stripes nor the incompetence for giving evidence is cancelled by repentance but that it removes only the spiritual stigma of being regarded as a "wicked transgressor".

Accusation of one Spouse by the Other
If a husband puts forward an accusation against his wife or a wife against her husband, the Holy Qur'an lays down the following procedure:

**And for those who launch a charge against their spouses, and
have (in support) no evidence but their own,
their solitary evidence can be received
if they bear witness four times with an oath by Allah that they
are solemnly telling the truth.
And a fifth (oath) should be that they solemnly invoke the curse
of Allah on themselves if they tell a lie.
But it would avert the punishment from the wife
if she bears witness four times with (an oath) by Allah that he
(her husband) is telling a lie.**

**And the fifth (oath) should be that she solemnly invokes the
wrath of Allah on herself
if (her accuser) is telling the truth. (24:5-9)**

In the context of the permission granted by Islam to a husband
to divorcing his wife, the case of accusation of the wife by the
husband takes an entirely different colour from what it has in the
western legal system. In Western countries, the spouse who decides
to obtain a divorce has to plead that the other spouse is guilty of
adultery and only on the basis of this plea can divorce be granted by
court of law. This was necessarily a potent reason for making false
accusations. But in Islam even if a Muslim catches his wife in an
actual act of adultery, which is not generally possible, it is still
necessary for him to produce four witnesses who have seen the act
itself. In most cases it will be difficult to find witnesses. Therefore,
the husband will have to swear in the Shari'ah court four times to
the act of his wife's adultery and in addition invoke a curse on
himself if he is not telling the truth. It will be a *prima facie* proof of
the wife's guilt. If the wife similarly swears her innocence four
times and then she invokes a curse on herself if she is not telling the
truth, she will be acquitted of the charge. But if she refuses to take
the oaths, the charge will be deemed proved against her and she will
have to face the punishment.

Whatever happens, once the oaths are taken, the marriage will
be dissolved since it is quite impossible that the spouses would ever
be able to live in peace and harmony after such an experience.

According to Abu Zayd al-Qayrawani al-Maliki, there can be no
hadd punishment of minors either in respect of levelling a false
accusation of unchastity (*qadhf*) or in respect of committing
fornication. Anybody who denies the paternity of another will
receive the *hadd* punishment. Accusations of unchastity are always
given the *hadd* punishment - even if they are made by using
innuendoes. If a man says to another, "O you homosexual!" he also
receives the *hadd* punishment. If a man levels a false accusation
against a group of people, he receives one *hadd* punishment if all of
them demand it. Afterwards he is free and guiltless.

If a man drinks wine repeatedly or commits adultery repeatedly,
he is only to receive only one *hadd* punishment in respect of all the
repeated offences. This rule applies in respect of the person who
levels false accusations against a group of people. If a person is

liable to receive *hadd* punishments and at the same time liable to be executed, the execution alone is sufficient for all the offences except where the *hadd* punishment is in respect of adultery. Under such circumstances, the man must receive the *hadd* punishment and then be executed afterwards.

7
FAMILY PLANNING AND ABORTION

The use of artificial contraceptives was unheard of in the time of the Prophet, the Rashidun khalifs, and the early Muslim empires. Hence our discussion on this subject will be limited to the modern methods of family planning and contraception and whether they are lawful or otherwise according to the Islamic Shari'ah.

Children are in reality the joy of a family. Childbirth is considered as one of the objectives of the institution of marriage in Islam. But there are certain circumstances when a child is not welcome:

(1) If child-bearing is going to endanger the life of the mother or there is a danger envisaged to the life of the mother at the time of delivery. The above points have their justification in the following verses of the Qur'an:

Do not throw yourself into destruction
with your own hands. (2:195)

Do not destroy yourselves;
undoubtedly Allah is merciful to you. (4:29)

(2) If there is any fear of getting involved in some special financial, educational or other problems in respect of children which would stop a man from fulfilling his religious duties .

(3) If it forces a man to accept unlawful things or unlawful food just for the sake of his children. The justification for this lies in the following verses of the Qur'an:

Allah wants to ease your problems;
He does not want to be harsh upon you. (2:184)

Allah does not want to force
any hardship upon you. (5:6)

(4) If there is a danger of ruining the health of the children. If the

father or mother is suffering from a contagious disease which can be transmitted to the children, but this will certainly not apply to hereditary diseases like diabetes and other such diseases.

(5) If there is a danger to that the parents would not be in a position to give proper training(*tarbiyyah*) to the children as required by Islam.

The above stipulations occur in the following *hadith* of the Prophet which speaks of withdrawal at the time of ejaculation so that no drop of semen could be deposited in the vaginal passage of the wife:

"It is narrated by Usama that a man came to the Prophet and said, 'O Messenger of Allah! I separate myself away from my wife during sexual intercourse *(al-'uzl)*.' The Prophet then asked, 'Why do you do so?' The man replied that he did so that he might not harm the child. The Prophet then replied, 'If there was any truth about harming the child, the people of Persia and Rome would suffer from the same harm.' " [Sahih Muslim]

In other words, the above *hadith* speaks of at least one method of contraception or family planning practised during the days of the Prophet. It can be derived from this *hadith* that if there is real danger to the health of the child, this action of *'uzla* which amounts to interrupting coitus at the moment of male ejaculation, is justifiable. One such justification is that it can harm a nursing child who is being given suck by his mother if she becomes pregnant again. In such cases, the mother's milk loses nutritive value and the child is more liable to weakness and disease. The above *hadith* is further strengthened by another *hadith* narrated by Abu Da'ud:

"Do not destroy your children in a concealed way since having intercourse with one's wife while she is giving suck to a child harms the child." [Abu Da'ud]

But this wise counsel of the Prophet should not be misconstrued as a forbidding command of the Prophet. If sexual intercourse during the period of giving suck to the child was completely forbidden by the Prophet, it would have put husbands to a great deal of inconvenience since the period of suck lasts for two years. Those who can afford to maintain more than one wife with all equity and justice as demanded by Islam will take the polygamous way of life. But this is not possible for everyone. Taking all these human problems into consideration, the Prophet said:

"I wanted to forbid (make it *haram*) sexual intercourse with mothers who are giving suck to their children, but I have come to know about the people of Persia and Rome that they do so and their children are not really harmed." [Sahih Muslim]

The great scholar, Ibn Qayyim, has analysed and explained the two *hadiths* and interpreted them jointly in the following words:

"There were two different situations resulting from having sexual intercourse with a nursing mother. One was that it would be harmful to the child if sexual intercourse took place with the nursing mother. Although this harm was not in any way comparable to the crime of killing or murdering the child, still, because of the possible harm to the child, the Prophet forbade sexual intercourse with the mother. But this restriction does not become part of declaring it unlawful *(haram)*. The Prophet also wanted to forbid this act in order to bar the way to harm occurring *(sadd adh-dhari'ah)*. But then the other aspect came before the Prophet, that by forbidding sexual intercourse with the mother for such a period other evils might come into existence - like adultery and prostitution. It can particularly affect young people and passionate individuals who might fall easy prey to adultery and prostitution. Therefore the Prophet said that sexual intercourse with nursing mothers should be allowed. Besides, the practice of the two great nations of that time was also before the Prophet and hence the Prophet did not declare sexual intercourse with a nursing mother forbidden."[1]

The above prophetic traditions and the interpretation of Ibn Qayyim gives us enough guidance in respect of modern contraceptive methods. These include various contraceptive pills and other devices. By the use of such methods one can prevent harm to the child who is being given suck by the mother. It can also stop the danger of adultery and prostitution since the young and passionate can still go to their wives during the period of giving suck to their children. Here it is essential to point out that surgical sterilization which involves an operation in which certain veins are cut is not included in the above permissible contraceptive methods since it involves changing human physiology as created by Allah *(taghyir fi khalq Allah)*. Sterilization or other forms of operations are *haram* (unlawful) since they amount to mutilation of the human body. The great jurists have given their opinions about *'uzl* (coitus interruptus) which can only be done with the permission of the wife. Imam Ahmad ibn Hanbal is of the opinion that it must never be done without the wife's permission since she has every right to have a child as well as sexual satisfaction. The Khalif 'Umar forbade the practice of 'uzl without the permission of the wife.

Is Birth Control Permissable in the Shari'ah?

So far we have discussed the use of contraception in order to avoid greater harm to Muslim parents. Present day contraceptives are used primarily as a deliberate measure to obstruct the fertilisation of the human egg in order to curtail the frequency of births either as a measure introduced by various governments in the Muslim as well as the non-Muslim world, or as a fashion copied from the Western world. Pills and IUDs are themost frequent methods used since they have proved to be most effective in the prevention of birth.

From the point of view of Islamic Law, the practice of birth control without any of the legitimate reasons that we have discussed before is not allowed since it amounts to losing one's trust and faith in Allah. Birth control movements are generally based on an unfounded fear that the population increase will result in scarcity of food for the human race in the world. But Allah's lands are vast, and many food resources such as the seaweeds which are highly nutritive have not been explored as yet.

The vast areas of waste land lying untouched in the world have great potentialities once brought under cultivation. Modern technology and expert hands can convert them into fertile lands to provide food for millions of people. The Malthusian theory of population which says that food stuffs and other necessities grow by arithmetical progression while the population grows by exponetial progression has been proved wrong in recent times. Likewise the other theories which give a grim picture of the world if population growth is allowed will equally be proved wrong as time goes on.

Unless contraceptives are used in the legitimate situations we have discussed before, they are in fact unlawful. There are some apologetic Muslim scholars who feel that this is 'an exaggerated view', and labour to explain that lawful fertilization of the ovum depends upon a number of steps, none of which is a mandatory obligation. These include marriage, intercourse, and continuation of it till ejaculation. Moreover, masturbation, which is a deliberate waste of the fertilizing force, is said to be permissible when fornication is otherwise feared, according to some jurists. General prohibition conflicts with these realities.[2]

In reality, fornication and masturbation are two different things altogether. Fornication is *zina,* a great crime in the Shari'ah, and highly injurious to the *ummah* and corrupts society as a whole. Masturbation is something personal and at the most one resorts to it at the risk of one's own health. It has no repercussions on others whatsoever. It is also an evil, but a very minor one compared to *zina.*

Pills and IUDs also have some dangerous side effects, and one resorts to these contraceptives at one's own risk, only in legitimate situations. According to the established principle of the Shari'ah, if there is a choice between two necessary evils, the lesser evil must be chosen.

Abortion as a Means of Family Planning

Islam forbids abortion completely in family planning, and it is considered a murderous crime. Once pregnancy has taken place, it must not be harmed in any circumstances. Any harm caused to the pregnancy amounts to harm caused to the child in embryo. All the jurists of the four schools of Islamic jurisprudence have reached consensus on this issue: that abortion after life has been infused in the embryo is unlawful and amounts to the crime of taking a life. Once the pregnancy reaches four months, it is medically proven, just as the great jurists of the four schools indicated a long time ago, that the embryo becomes a fully-fledged child.

If the pregnancy is aborted alive, apart from being a great crime, it becomes obligatory to pay *diyah* (blood-money) in Islamic law. If the pregnancy is extracted dead, fines have to be imposed which are less than the amount of the *diyah.* In spite of taking the *diyah,* or fine, the crime still remains a crime if the abortion is performed without any strict medical reasons, such as a real threat to the life of the expectant mother.

Supposing that on medical grounds it becomes essential to perform an abortion in order to save the life of the mother then the abortion would be allowed. The Shari'ah stipulates that when you have to deal with two harmful matters, the less harmful should be adopted. The main life is the life of the mother as she is alive and has a right to live. Hence the life of the living mother must not be sacrificed for the sake of the life of the embryo.[3]

Use of contraceptive methods to prevent pregnancy is quite a different issue from procuring an abortion. The contraceptive methods do not amount to the murder or killing of the child since the child does not come into existence at all when preventative methods are used.

8
EQUALITY OF LEGAL RIGHTS FOR WOMEN

Men and women are treated equally in all branches of Islamic law. The concept of equality of treatment is not confined to mere theories, but is practised in the courts by *qadis*. If a man injures a woman or kills her, he will be dealt with very severely under the Shari'ah. It is this strict code of conduct which keeps the crime rate to the minimum. The Shari'ah protects the rights to life and safety of both men and women. If any man murders a woman, the *hadd* punishment of *qisas* will be applied to him, and he will be killed. Likewise, a woman murderer will be put to death according to the following Qur'anic injunction on equitable retaliation:

**There is life for you in *qisas*,
O people of intelligence. (2:179)**

Thus it can be seen that a woman's life is absolutely as respected and sacred as the life of a man. If anyone spills the blood of another, their own blood becomes lawful to be spilt. When the Prophet had the law written for the Yemenites, it was especially mentioned that..."undoubtedly a man will be killed for killing a woman." [1]

A Jew killed a girl by crushing her head in the time of the Prophet. The Messengeer of Allah ordered him to be killed in the same way.[2] The Khalif 'Umar put to death a number of persons who were accomplices to the murder of a woman.[3] Imam al-Bayhaqi reported in his *as-Sunan al-Kubra* on the authority of Sa'id ibn al-Musayyib, 'Urwah ibn az-Zubayr, Qasim ibn Muhammad, Abu Bakr ibn 'Abdu'r-Rahman and others:

"They used to say (in the matter of *qisas*) that there is no difference between a man and a woman. In the matter of injuries to a woman's eyes, ears, or any other kinds of wounds, the *qisas* operates in the same way as in the case of a man. If a man kills a woman he is to be killed.[4] Similarly, if a woman forgives the murderer of her nearest relative by accepting *diyah*, nobody is entitled to reject her decision."

If the guardians of the murdered person differ on the point of accepting *diyah* and forgiving him, the other relatives are prevented from taking his life. It is immaterial if the person forgiving happens to be a man or a woman.[5] Abu Da'ud in his *Kitab al-Jihad* says: "It is reported by 'A'ishah that a woman can provide refuge during the period of war and the refuge will be accepted."

It is well-known that during the conquest of Makka Umm Hani', 'Ali's sister, said to the Prophet that she had given refuge to Ibn Hira. 'Ali insisted on killing the enemy, but the Prophet intervened, "O Umm Hani'! Whosoever you have given refuge to has also received our refuge." (Al-Bukhari, *Kitab al-Jihad*)

Women's Political Rights

Islam is the religion of this world (*din ad-dunya*) and the religion of the Next World (*din al-akhirah*). Hence women have a say in deciding the affairs of the state in which they live. The lawful affairs of this world in this case are also be treated as affairs of religion.[7] What is the Islamic point of view about a woman occupying positions like ministerhip[8] judgeship[9] leadership in *jihad*[10] leadership in resolving public complaints[11] and the police force?[12] These positions are meant for the dual purpose: helping both the religion and the defence of the country.

The jurists differ in their opinions about giving women all the above positions. However, there are some jurists who feel that, if need arises, women should be given these positions. All the jurists, however, agree that a woman should not be appointed to the position of Khalif.[13] Since the khalifate no longer exists in the Muslim world, this principle also applies to a woman's appointment as the Head of State. Since there are complicated issues to be handled, both religious and political, it may be difficult for a woman to handle them, taking into consideration the strict code of modesty and conduct given by the religion of Islam and the biological make-up of a woman.[14]

The Messenger of Allah said, "A nation will not prosper if it is led by a woman."

The only sect in Islam which allowed the headship of a woman is a now non-existent branch of the Kharijites which was once known as ash-Shuhaybiyyah.[16] The belief of this sect was outside the consensus of the opinion of the jurists (*ijma'*).[17]

Likewise, the consensus of opinion of the jurists is that a woman is not eligible to become a minister by the same conditions and arguments as we have seen in respect of the position of Khalif.[18]

The same principle applies to the leadership of a province, leadership in the battlefield, judicial positions and positions in the complaints commission and the police force. Imam Abu Hanifah, the founder of the Hanafi school of jurisprudence, says that a woman can be appointed to a judicial position where she is supposed to adjudicate in civil and commercial cases, but he too says that it is not proper to appoint her to a position where she is supposed to adjudicate in *hadd* punishment and equitable retaliation[19] cases and cases involving *nikah*. However, scholars like Ibn Jarir at-Tabari have said that a woman can be appointed to a judicial position to adjudicate in all matters.[20]

9

WOMEN AND EDUCATION

The Holy Prophet made women integral to his plan for Muslim education and learning when he declared:
"Acquisition of knowledge is obligatory for every Muslim, male and female."

Women were encouraged to study the Qur'an and the *Sunnah* and the Arabic language in the time of the Prophet.

'A'ishah says, "In the time of the Prophet, may Allah bless him and grant him peace, whenever any verse was revealed, we used to memorize the lawful, the unlawful, the do's and the don'ts contained in it, even if we did not memorize its exact words."[1]

'A'ishah used to praise the women of the *Ansar* (the Helpers of the Prophet in Madina) in the following words, "How good were the women of the Ansar that they did not shy away from learning and comprehending religious matters." (Muslim, *Kitab al-Hayd*)

The women in the time of the Prophet had become so keen to acquire more knowledge that they came to the Prophet with the following proposal:

"The womenfolk said to the Prophet, 'You are always surrounded by men, so appoint a day for us.' The Prophet promised to do so and went to them and taught them." (Al-Bukhari, *Kitab al-'Idayn*)

The Prophet not only took this important function upon himself, but also sent his representatives with messages to enlighten the Muslim women. This is borne out by the following tradition:

"It is reported by Umm 'Atiyyah that when the Messenger of Allah came to Madina, he ordered the women of the *Ansar* to gather in one house and sent 'Umar ibn al-Khattab to them (for conveying the teachings of Islam). He saluted them while standing at the door of the house. They returned his greeting. Then he said, 'I am a messenger of the Messenger of Allah sent specially to you.' " (Al-Bukhari)

The Holy Prophet made it a point of duty for every father and mother to make sure that their daughters did not remain ignorant of the teachings of Islam because they would, after their marriage, have to play important roles as housewives and as mothers of children.

In case the parents had failed to impart such knowledge to their daughters, it was made incumbent upon husbands to teach their wives the basic principles so that they would lead their lives according to the teachings of Islam.

It is reported that Malik ibn Huwayrith and a group of young men had come to live near the Prophet and acquire knowledge from him.

When they decided to return to their respective homes, the Prophet told them, "Return home to your wives and children and stay with them. Teach them (what you have learnt) and ask them to act upon it." (Al-Bukhari)

There is an interesting incident showing how great an importance is attached to learning in Islam. Once a poor companion of the Holy Prophet wanted to marry a woman. But he did not possess anything to give her by way of dowry (*mahr*). However, he had thoroughly learned some *surahs* (Chapters of the Qur'an). The Prophet, peace be upon him, married the woman to him on condition that he would teach those chapters to her and said that his labour in teaching would be his dowry. (Al-Bukhari)

It is on this basis that a great Maliki jurists, Ibn al-Hajj, expressed the following view:

"If a woman demands her right to religious education from her husband, and brings the issue before a judge she is justified in demanding this right because it is her right that either her husband should teach her or allow her to go elsewhere to acquire education. The judge must compel the husband to fulfil her demand in the same way that he would in the matter of her worldly rights since her right in matters of religion are most essential and important."[2]

A similar view was also expressed by an eminent Hanafi jurist, Fakhr al-Din Hasan ibn Mansur. [3]

The result of the importance that the Holy Prophet attached to the education of Muslim women was that a marked change was brought about in Arabian society. Women who only a few years before had been looked down upon as mere chattels unfit for education or learning, became among the most learned figures of their time and started offering guidance to others in educational matters. A number of such women can be mentioned as follows:

Some Great Muslim Women Scholars

'A'isha Bint Abu Bakr

The consequences of this teaching of Islam in respect of education of women were very surprising in what had been the pagan society of the *Jahiliyyah* Arabs who simply hated women and looked down upon them as mere chattels. The women of Arabia, who until the advent of Islam had been completely unaware of learning and literature, became the protectors of learning and offered guidance to others in this respect.

The first and foremost example is that of 'A'ishah, the wife of the Prophet, who lived long after her husband's death and provided great guidance to the first Muslim community, even to the renowned *Sahabah* and the *Rashidun* Khalifs. Her pupil, 'Urwah ibn az-Zubayr, testifies to her high place in learning in the following words recorded in *Tadhkirah al-Huffaz*:

"I did not see a greater scholar than 'A'ishah in the learning of the Qur'an, obligatory duties, lawful and unlawful matters, poetry and literature, Arab history and genealogy."[4]

'Urwah ibn az-Zubayr was himself a great scholar of literature. When he was praised once, he said that he was nothing compared to 'A'ishah who could quote couplets of verse in every discussion. Musa ibn Talha, another great contemporary *Sahabi* says: "I have not seen anyone more eloquent than 'A'ishah."[5]

Others also observed her proficiency in various fields of learning and praised her highly. Ibn Abi Malikah said that we should not be surprised by her authority in the matter of poetry since she was the daughter of Abu Bakr who himself was very eloquent and a great literary figure; but what is surprising is her profound knowledge of medicine. Whenever the foreign delegations came to the Prophet and discussed various remedies for illnesses, she used to remember them. She was so well versed in mathematics that important *Sahabah* used to consult her on the problems concerning *mirath* (inheritance) and the calculation of the shares.

Her reputation as a scholar spread far and wide. People came from different places to ascertain about *ahadith* of the Prophet that they had heard from different scholars. As we notice in the manuals of a *hadith.*, 'A'ishah even guided *Sahabah* who sought her advice on different matters. They included the *Khalif* 'Umar, 'Abdullah ibn 'Umar, and Abu Hurayrah. She was among the great *huffaz* (memorisers) of *ahadith*. She narrated 2210 *ahadith* in all.

No other *Sahabi* narrated so many *ahadith* except 'Abdullah ibn

'Umar, Anas and Abu Hurayrah. The great *Sahabah* of the Prophet usually referred to 'A'ishah whenever they had any difficulty in understanding any juristic problem. Abu Musa al-Ash'ari, himself a famous jurist and learned scholar, says, "Whenever we Companions of the Prophet, may Allah bless him and grant him peace, encountered any difficulty in the matter of any *hadith* we referred it to 'A'ishah and found that she had definite knowledge about it."

Knowledge gained from 'A'ishah was so authentic that the famous jurist of Madina, 'Urwah ibn az-Zubayr, and the famous *muhaddith* Qasim ibn Muhammad always gave juristic opinions on the authority of the narrations of 'A'ishah. Ahmad ibn Hanbal writes, "These two were among those who relied on the authority of the narrations of 'A'ishah, and did not digress from her statements, and gave their juristic opinions based on the narrations of 'A'ishah."

'A'ishah had a very sharp memory and remembered the teachings of the Prophet very well. She survived the Prophet, living for fifty years after him and teaching a large number of people who all benefited from her. Hafiz ibn Hajar says about her in *Fath al-Bari*:

"'A'ishah remembered many teachings of the Prophet and survived for fifty years after him. People learnt a lot from her and narrated many injunctions and etiquettes from her, to the extent that it is said that one fourth of the injunctions of the *Shari'ah* are narrated from her."

Hafiz ibn Hajar gives the names of eighty-eight great scholars who learnt from her, and then says that there were a large number of others. These include great politicians like 'Amr ibn al-'As, Abu Musa al-Ash'ari and 'Abdullah ibn az-Zubayr; great jurists and scholars of a *hadith* like Abu Hurayrah, 'Abdullah ibn 'Abbas and 'Abdullah ibn 'Umar; and great scholars amongst the *Tabi'un* like Sa'id ibn al-Musayyab and 'Alqamah ibn Qays.[6]

Saffiyah: Wife of the Prophet

Safiyyah, the wife of the Prophet, was also very learned in *fiqh*. Suhayrah bint Jaifar says, "Some of us went to Madina after performing the *hajj* and paid a visit to Safiyyah. We found a group of women learning from her. They had come from Kufah. We also learnt from her many things concerning family relations and menstruation, etc."[7] Allah alone knows how many groups must have benefited from Safiyyah's knowledge.

Imam an-Nawawi says, "She was the most intellectual the

among learned women."[8]

Umm Salamah: Wife of the Prophet
She was also a great scholar. The scholar, Ibn Hajar, has given the names of at least thirty-two great scholars who learnt *ahadith* from her, and then narrated them on her authority. Marwan and many like him turned to her to learn various *fiqh* issues. He used to say, "Why should we turn to others when we have the Prophet's wives among us?"

Ibn Hajar writes about Umm Salamah, "Umm Salamah was gifted with great beauty, mature intellect and wisely-guided opinions." [9]

Rabi'ah Bint Mu'awwad
She was also a great scholar of *fiqh*. The learned scholars of Madina like 'Abdullah ibn 'Abbas, 'Abdullah ibn 'Umar, Salman ibn Yasar, 'Abbad ibn Walid and Nafi' used to go to her to learn from her. [10]

Umm 'Atiyyah
Umm 'Atiyyah was also a great scholar. According to 'Allamah ibn 'Abd al-Barr, she was present at the funeral *ghusl* of the daughter of the Holy Prophet. She narrated the incident in great detail.

Some *Sahabah* and learned scholars among the *Tabi'un* used to come to her to learn various aspects of Islamic jurisprudence from her in Basrah. She also narrated many *ahadith* of the Prophet. Imam an-Nawawi said about her, "She was a scholarly *Sahabiyah*, and one of those who went on *jihad* with the Messenger of Allah." [11]

'A'isha Bint Sa'd Ibn Abi Waqqas
She was the daughter of a great *Sahabi*, Sa'd ibn Abi Waqqas. She was very learned in Islamic sciences, to such an extent that Imam Malik, Hakam ibn 'Utaybah and Ayyub as-Sakhtiyani, the famous jurists and scholars of *hadith* were her pupils.

Sayyida Nafisa: Granddaughter of Hasan
She was a great scholar. A large number of pupils came to her from different places to learn from her. Imam Shafi'i, founder of the Shafi'i school of Islamic law, was one of her illustrious pupils. [12]

'Umrah Bint 'Abdu'r-Rahman

One of the illustrious pupils of 'A'ishah was 'Umrah bint 'Abdu'r-Rahman who was described by Ahmad ibn Hanbal in the following words, "An eminent theologian and a great scholar. 'Umrah ibn 'Abdu'r-Rahman was tutored in the lap of 'A'ishah. She narrated many *ahadith* from her. She is very reliable, had an excellent memory and is one whose narration can be accepted."

Ibn Habban also calls her a great scholar in the *ahadith* related by 'A'ishah, "She was the most learned of all pupils in the *ahadith* of 'A'ishah." [13]

'Umar ibn 'Abdu'l-'Aziz, the great Umayyad Khalif who is rightly described by historians as one who was of the calibre of the *Khulafa' ar-Rashidun*, respected the narrations of 'Umrah bint 'Abdu'r-Rahman to such an extent that he asked Abu Bakr ibn Muhammad ibn Hazm to record them. Hence great scholars like Abu Bakr ibn Hazm, Imam az-Zuhri and Yahya ibn Sa'id, all of whom were great jurists, went to 'Umrah to learn *ahadith* from her.

Zaynab: The Daughter of Umm Salamah

Umm Salamah herself was a great and learned lady as we have discussed before but her daughter, Zaynab, was also an expert in the field of jurisprudence. Ibn 'Abdu'l-Barr says about her, "She was a theologian of greater status than others of her contemporaries." [14]

Umm Ad-Darda': Wife of Abu'd-Darda'

Umm ad-Darda', the wife of the famous *Sahabi* Abu ad-Darda', was so learned in the science of *hadith* that Imam al-Bukhari, one of the compilers of the *Sihah as-Sittah* (the six canonical collections of Hadith) referred to her as an authority in his *Sahih al-Bukhari:* "Umm ad-Darda' used to sit (in *tashahhud*) in her prayers like a man and she was an expert theologian (hence her action is worth emulating)."

Ibn 'Abdu'l-Barr calls her "an excellent scholar among women, and a woman intellectual, being at the same time extremely religious and pious." [16]

Imam an-Nawawi has said that "...all scholars are unanimously agreed regarding her vast knowledge of *fiqh*, her intelligence, her profound understanding and her greatness." [17]

Fatimah Bint Qays

Fatimah bint Qays was also a scholarly lady in the early days of Islam. Her learning was so deep that she discussed a juristic point with 'Umar and 'A'ishah for a long time and they also could not change or challenge her views. Imam an-Nawawi says, "She was one of those who migrated in the early days, and possessed great intellect and excellence." [18]

Umm Salim: Mother of Anas

Umm Salim, the mother of the famous *Sahabi* Anas, was herself a highly respected *Sahabiyah*. Hafiz Ibn Hajar praises her, saying, "Her laudable qualities are too many to mention and she was very famous."

Imam an-Nawawi calls her "an excellent scholar among the *Sahabiyah*." [19]

This list of learned women of the early days of Islam shows that women were not kept illiterate and ignorant, but rather were fully encouraged to participate in the process of learning and scholarship. They also knew their rights and responsibilities very well. There were instances to show that some women even challenged great scholars of their times if they said something which was against the rights granted to women by the Qur'an and the *Sunnah*.

Facilities for the Education of Muslim Women

Any discussion about the education of women would not be complete without considering what type of facilities should be provided so that Muslim women may not only acquire knowledge but also combine it with the high moral qualities that Islam seeks to inculcate in the future mothers of the *Ummah*.

So far as religious knowledge is concerned, its acquisition is obligatory for both men and women. But even in the case of education in other branches of human knowledge, there is absolutely no prohibition in the Prophetic tradition regarding its acquisition by women. Therefore Muslim women have every right to go to secondary schools and universities in the present educational system provided proper arrangements are made for them to receive instruction without free mixing with male students.

Whatever trumpets the proponents of co-education may blow in praise of the system of co-education, the sad fact remains that a majority of the girl students in the secondary schools in Europe and America spend more time in picking up illicit sexual techniques from their male classmates than in collecting useful knowledge from their teachers. The position of women studying in colleges and universities is even worse in the sense that there are cases of lecturers and professors harassing them into submitting to their demands for sex before these unfortunate girls can get good grades in their examinations.

Newsweek magazine recently brought out a report about abuse of female students in the American Universities.[20] It contains the following paragraph, "The psychological drain can be particularly severe in a university. 'There needs to be a relationship of trust and even intimacy between students and professors,' says attorney Catherine A, 'Sexual harassment can destroy even the possibility of learning.' Affairs between professors and students have long been the subject of campus jokes, but women aren't laughing any more. Harvard, Yale and the University of California are among the institutions where formal charges have been filed. A law-suit alleging that a Yale Political Science professor promised an 'A' grade in return for sexual intercourse is now pending in the Federal Appeals Court."

Therefore we should dispense with the system of co-education and should open primary schools, secondary schools, colleges and universities exclusively for women where the teachers as well as the students are women. The uniform for all female students should satisfy the requirements laid down by the *Shari'ah* for proper dress.

It is encouraging to note that countries like Saudi Arabia, Iran and Pakistan, have recently started specialist educational institutions for women up to university level on this pattern. King 'Abdu'l-'Aziz University in Jeddah has even set up a medical college for women having only women teachers. It is now high time that Muslims gave up their inferiority complex and tried to evolve a new educational system which is more in line with their own method and heritage. Where there is a will there is a way.

10

ECONOMIC RIGHTS OF WOMEN IN THE SHARI'AH

Lawful and Unlawful Employment for Muslim Women

We have already discussed the point that the roles of the spouses are biologically determined. Islam reaffirms this differentiation andprescribes specific basic rules for socialization as follows [1] :

(1) The family is a vital mechanism for the sane structure of society. It must be based on legitimate marriage.

(2) It is the law of creation that in every grouping there must be order. In animals in general and in man in particular, there must always be a leader, for every herd, for every flock and for every social or political formation.

(3) There are moral and legal rights and obligations that come into force when marriage takes place. Unless both are accepted with conviction and contentment, no happy family relationship can result. The main moral values of an Islamic marriage are unity and sharing, always keeping the main purpose of marriage in view. When these moral values are adopted, the question of "equality" becomes invalid because it does not arise. Man and women are treated equally by their Creator and are subject to the same transactional and behaviourial views expressed in the Qur'an.

(4) Because of their different physiological structures and biological functions, each sex is assigned a role to play in the family. This role is compatible with and emanates from their respective biological formations.

In the olden days, women everywhere looked after their home and family and did not leave home. Arnold J. Toynbee, the renowed author of the famous "Study of History", said, "Certainly our recent efforts to solve our problems in strictly materialist terms have failed and made caricatures of all our brave plans. We have made enormous strides in the development of labour-saving machinery but one of the odd results of this progress is that women today are overworked as never before. Wives in America can no longer get household help or afford to devote themselves exclusively to the home.

As a result, the woman of today does two jobs: one as wife in the home; and the other as employee in the office or factory. In fifth century Greece, the high point of classical history, women stayed in the home. But after Alexander's time when the city states were breaking up, there was a feminist movement like our own."2 Once women started going out to work it increased their independence. In modern times, it has become almost impossible to ask women not to go out to work.

Islam does not require women to participate in trade, the vocations or professions unless it is very necessary. As we have seen earlier, the realm of activities for which men and women are created requires a woman to look after her matrimonial home, bring up children in a befitting manner and so on. If she is not neglectful of these duties, or she has reliable household help available to look after her children and relieve her of some of her domestic work, while at the same time she needs a little income to supplement her husband's earning, there is no objection in the Shari'ah if she goes out to work, but only with the consent of her husband.

The jobs that she undertakes to do must be lawful. She must not work as a dancer, a model, a barmaid, a waitress, a film actress, a musician or a prostitute to sell her feminity in order to make money, even with the consent of her husband. Apart from these, all other work and professions are lawful if Muslim women adhere to Islamic principles in respect of dress and modesty.

Secretarial Work

Secretarial positions which women proudly accept nowadays often require them to sit solitarily in an office surrounded by men or in their boss's office where they are continually alone with him. We hear of many cases where the secretary becomes a keeper of her boss's secrets and ultimately becomes his mistress. According to a *hadith*, when a man and woman sit alone anywhere, Satan, whose work is to beguile mankind, makes a third person. If the people employed are exclusively women, there is no harm in accepting a secretarial position.

Factory Work

A Muslim woman can work in a factory if it is run by women. In modern factories in Europe, America and in Third World Countries, even in some Muslim countries, men and women work together in factories. This is grossly un-Islamic. But, if factories are constructed especially for them, or two arms of a factory are created, one for men and the other for women, it can be more effective and productive. Islamic law does not stop women working in factories if proper conditions are created for them as required by the system of Islamic values.

Market Trading

Trading by a woman is not forbidden in the Shari'ah. On the contrary, we have quite a few examples of women in the early centuries of Islam engaged in lawful trading, operating within the strict code of conduct of Islam. A woman's trade and business must not take her to the marketplace where she will have to intermingle with her male counterparts. In the first place, the market can lure away even a pious man from his complete reliance on Allah if he is involved in unlawful trade practice. In one *hadith* the Prophet described the marketplace as the worst place and the mosque as the best place for members of the *ummah*.

In some countries there are young girls who hawk in the streets with petty merchandise which is carried on their heads as can be seen in most countries of West Africa. The scene is quite common among the Yoruba Muslim girls and Fulani milk-sellers. This practice is utterly un-Islamic as one can see many vices spreading within the free movement of women traders. Among the Yoruba, most businesses are run in the open market by Muslim women, but in most countries this is not the practice. But if women engage in trading in their own house where the buyers are small boys and girls from the neighbourhood there is absolutely no harm.

Other Kinds of Employment

Women can learn and establish small scale cottage industries in their homes or may engage in dress-designing and sewing. Some Muslim sisters in various cities in England and America have established sewing businesses in their homes while materials are supplied by businessmen dealing in garments. A friend's wife is making as much as £4000 from sewing dresses at home in London at the same time as looking after her matrimonial home and all the domestic responsibilities and ties connected with it. Women, while sitting at home, can gainfully employ themselves by preparing enamelware and pottery, dyeing and painting textiles, making baskets, making jewellery and ornaments, doing embroidery, knitting, etc.

Women in the Professions

Those women who are highly talented and have the opportunity to go to universities for higher education can render great services for the betterment of society., particularly in the teaching profession. But here too, a strict Islamic code of conduct has to be observed in the classroom. A Muslim woman can teach small children, whether male or female, in primary schools where the other teachers happen to be women. In the case of secondary schools and colleges and universities, they should be engaged to teach in girls' institutions only.

As for the medical profession, women doctors are badly needed in the field of gynaecology and obstetrics. Usually women feel shy and are even forbidden by the Shari'ah from consulting male doctors as far as possible in their ante-natal and post-natal treatment. But if it is a question of life and death, then under special circumstances they can consult a male doctor. Muslim ladies should be encouraged to join the medical profession and take up nursing as their career, but they should seek employment in female wards and hospitals.

Welfare Work

Women can be most effective in the juvenile courts and welfare institutions of our society. With their God-given touch of loving affection they can handle juvenile delinquents, drop-outs from schools or frustrated youths.

Working Women at the Time of the Prophet

It should be understood that a woman is not forbidden to go out of her home for essential work. In the time of the Prophet, women went out to the market or their farms. The Prophet did not stop a woman in her *'iddah* from going out of her house in the case of necessity. Jabir ibn 'Abdullah says that his aunt was divorced by her husband. Although she would have spent her *'iddah* in the house, she wanted to go out to get some of her date palms harvested and sold.

Someone stopped her, saying that it was not lawful to go out of the house during the period of *'iddah*. She went to the Prophet to get his verdict. The Prophet replied, "You go out and get the date trees harvested (and sold) so that you may be able to do some other good work." [4]

The Shari'ah thus permits women in *'iddah* to go out if there is real need for it. The time of the harvest had come, and she felt she should get it done. The *Shari'ah*, as is clear from the above *hadith*, looks upon a woman to give in charity out of her property. After the verses of *hijab* were revealed, 'Umar once saw Saudah going out of the house. He stopped her and criticised her. She returned home and told the Prophet what had happened. Thereupon the Prophet said, "Undoubtedly Allah has permitted you to go out to fulfil your needs." [5]

The example of Jabir's aunt quoted above shows that women did farming and harvesting. Sahl ibn Sa'ad, another Companion of the Prophet, also mentions a woman who planted vegetables and prepared a sweet dish of it on Friday.[6] We come across the name of a *Sahabiyah* called Qilah who came to the Prophet to ask various questions on business practice, and said, "I am a woman who purchases goods and sells." [7]

During the khalifate of Sayyiduna 'Umar, a woman named Asma' bint Makhzumah used to get perfume from her son 'Abdullah ibn Rabi'ah from the Yemen and sell it.[8] Sayyiduna 'Ali once praised the purchasing skill of a woman called 'Umrah when she bought a big fish at a reasonable price.[9] Once the wife of a famous scholar, the *Sahabi* 'Abdullah ibn Mas'ud, complained to the Prophet, saying that she had very little income only from handicraft: "I am a woman engaged in handicraft (on which we survive), but my husband and my son have nothing." [10]

Abuse of Working Women

The idea of working women, so much in vogue in the Western world, has created the problems of sexual abuse in offices. There is frequent incidence of sexual harassment, either through the threat of dismissed or allurement and promises of promotion given by the boss. It is a common scene in offices, factories and working places that co-workers and bosses make off-colour jokes and at times there are incidents of direct imterference. As *Newsweek* put it in its detailed study of "Abusing Sex at the Office" in its issue of 17 March 1980, it is done in a manner as subtle as a leer and a series of off-colour jokes, or as direct as grabbing a woman's breast. It can be found in typing pools and factories, army barracks and legislative suites, city rooms and college lecture halls. It is fundamentally a man's problem, and exercise of power almost analogous to rape, for which women pay with their jobs and sometimes with their health.[11] *Newsweek* made a study of the following two cases showing how widespread sexual harassment on the job is in the United States of America:

"In Los Angeles, supermarket checker Hallie Edwards walked into a storeroom and found a manager exposing himself and groping for her breasts. After Edwards complained, the chairman promoted her boss and transferred her. In Cambridge, Mass., college freshman Helene Sahadi York went to her Harvard professor's office looking for research help. She found an instructor determined to kiss her. In New York, typist Doreen Romano's boss offered her a raise if she would sleep with him. When she refused, he fired her.

The *Newsweek* report further says: "For more than a year, the boss of Cathy Peter, a 37 year old secretary to a New Jersey school superintendent, repeatedly made passes at her. Because she needed the job, she did not complain. One day, he left a note on her desk describing the attributes of a good secretary. Among them: "neat appearance, slender in body and willing to go to bed with the boss, satisfaction guaranteed."

Looking at Western society, some sexual advances made by men in the office like pinching a woman or creating an atmosphere loaded with sexual innuendoes and jokes are not taken very seriously. What would amount to sexual harassment in Eastern countries is considered as "natural" in Western society. It is due to this reason that sexual harassment remains difficult to define in the Western world. But there too, there are women who are shy and sexual harassment can drive them to tranquillizers while other women may dismiss the sexual advances as merely innocent or manageable flirting. Grabbing a working woman or pinching her is not taken very seriously in most places in Europe and America.

If women in the Muslim world are allowed to work anywhere in any office or factory, even slight sexual abuse would amount to "adultery of the eyes", "adultery of the legs", "adultery of the hands" and so on and so forth. Islam does not look kindly upon a man flirting with a woman since this can ultimately result in sexual anarchy as happens in the Western world. Abuse of sex is not limited merely to men making advances to women. Not only women become victims. There are even cases of young men working under female bosses who become victims of sexual harassment. In the

case study by *Newsweek*, it was reported that: "John, 32, married
and a father, wanted to enroll in a federally funded training pro-
gramme. A higher-ranking woman offered to guarantee his admission if he would sleep with her. He did, two or three times, and she
provided the promised recommendation. But their relationship had
other costs. 'She made it very obvious in the office,' John says,
'She'd come over and say things like, "I'm looking forward to
tonight!" ' Hal, 31, a married Federal bureaucrat, found that his new
boss kept inviting him into her office where she would close the
door and load the conversation with sexual innuendoes. After two
months, she offered to become his sponsor in exchange for sex. 'She
was so blatant,' he says now after transferring to another agency, 'I
felt like it was a reversal of a 40's movie and I was Betty Grable.' "

The other evil consequence of women going out to work and
leaving their children, home and family uncared-for is that it ultimately results in the disintegration of their families. According to
Dr Sullivan, the author of the book, *Alcoholism*, "...the employment
of women in ordinary industrial occupations not only involves a
disorganisation of their domestic duties if they are married, but it
also interferes with the acquisition of the knowledge of household
duties in girlhood. The result is that appalling ignorance of everything connected with cookery, with cleanliness, with the management of children, which makes the average wife and mother in the
lower working classes in this country one of the most helpless and
thriftless of beings, and which therefore implies that the workman,
whose comfort depends on her, not only spends his free time in public houses, but also tends to make him take to alcohol. The types of
employment that withdraw women from domestic pursuits are likely to increase alcoholism and, it may be added, to increase its greatest potency for evil, namely its influence on the health of the
stock." [12]

Professor Khurshid Ahmad, while analysing the evils of impos-
ing upon women the obligation of earning their daily bread by
working laboriously in mills, factories, and farms, says that this
new role of women has proved in reality to be a great liability. It has
struck a fatal blow to family life and acute disintegration has set in.
The once noble institution of the family, the guardian of culture and
protector of civilization, has collapsed like a house of cards.
Women have abandoned it. Men dislike it. Streets have become centres of illegal activities; restaurants and parks become the places of

romantic ventures which further fans the flames of sexual desire. We have come to such a stage that George Ryley Scott says, "Today far more than ever before in the world's history there are for the finding large numbers of girls who are willing for all sorts of reasons to meet me halfway to sexual excitement and satisfaction. These are the amateur prostitutes of modern civilization." [13]

Although it may not happen with all working women, there may be a certain percentage of women who argue as to why should a woman who wins her own bread, supports herself economically and does not depend on anyone for security and maintenance, remain faithfully attached to only one man for the sake of satisfying her sexual desire? Why should she be prepared to subject herself to so many moral and legal curbs to shoulder the responsibilities of family life? Especially when the concept of moral equality has cleared her way of all obstacles for satisfying sexual desires freely. Why should she forsake the easy, pleasure-giving and alluring way of satisfying them and choose instead the antiquated way that is not only laden with responsibilities but demands sacrifices also? With the banishment of religion from life, the fear of committing sin has been automatically destroyed as we can see in western society today.

At the present time the Muslim *Ummah* should be asked, "Is there a real and genuine need for women to leave the confines of their homes in order to work?" In the majority of cases, it is the parents or husbands who encourage their daughters or wives to go out and work with a view to increasing the family income so that they may compete with their neighbours or friends in enjoying the luxuries of this modern way of life, even though it is at the risk of losing their family dignity and honour! On the other hand, some women take up jobs simply to escape the boredom of staying in empty homse during week-days.

There are, however, certain genuine cases (though only a few) where a family due to financial circumstances is compelled to send women out to work so that they can make ends meet. Why do the advocates of female emancipation not divert their time, energy and money to creating some sort of home-industries for women in Muslim countries?

With Islamic teachings on sex roles being what they are, has the Shari'ah made any alternative arrangement for women? The answer is in the affirmative. The economic rights of a Muslim woman can be summed up as follows:

(1) A woman is entitled to inherit from her father, her husband and her children.

(2) She is entitled to a *mahr* (dowry) from her husband which is a gift given at the time of marriage. However, it is obligatory and not optional and no limit is set as to its amount. It all depends on the financial means of the husband and the social status of the woman. All money or other property she gets from these or from other lawful sources belongs solely to her and her husband can claim no share in them according to Islamic law.

(3) She can, if she wishes, run her own lawful business within the bounds of Islamic teachings and keep the whole income to herself. Islamic law does not put any responsibility for domestic expenses on her.

(4) Allah orders husbands: "to retain their wives in kindness and to release them in kindness" in case of divorce. Therefore the dowry, the belongings and the right to receive maintenance during a period after divorce are fully granted to the wife by the Qur'anic injunctions, except in the case of adultery.

(5) If the husband dies, the wife's rights mentioned in the marriage contracts have a priority in settlement of his property.

These Islamic rights have been granted by the Shari'ah to give a woman economic security within marriage and after its dissolution either by divorce or by the death of the husband.

As Professor Khurshid Ahmad stresses, the status of woman in Islam with regard to inheritance, property, marriage and divorce is much higher than in other religions. The world must know and accept the truth that no other faith has given womenfolk so many rights and preserved their honour and chastity as Islam has done.

With this background in mind, we shall now proceed to examine a Muslim woman's rights of *mahr* (dowry), *mirath* (inheritance) in detail. We have already discussed a Muslim woman's rights to *nafaqa*.

Mahr (Dowry)

Mahr (dowry) is mentioned in the Holy Qur'an (4:4) as an essential part of Muslim marriage. It is given by the bridegroom to his bride in accordance with a mutual agreement. It may be of any value from a quarter of a dinar to a thousand dinars or more. *Mahr* is not the same as the African custom of giving a bride-price since marriage in Islam is not the sale of a bride to her husband. It also differs from the old European system of dowry in which a father used to give his daughter a large dowry at the time of marriage which became the property of the husband as if it was an inducement for him to marry the girl. The same is practised among the Christians and Hindus in Kerala and other parts of India. Fathers are required to pay very large dowries to find suitable husbands for their daughters. In the Arab *Jahiliyyah* society, *mahr* was considered as the property of the girl's guardian.

In Islam, on the other hand, *mahr* is a marriage gift from the bridegroom to his bride which becomes her exclusive property. Islam has elevated the status of women as *mahr* is given as a mark of respect for her. Even if the marriage ends in divorce the dowry remains the wife's property and the husband has no right to take it back, except in the case of *khul'* where the divorce takes place at the request of the wife in consideration of the return of the whole or part of the *mahr* paid to her at the time of her marriage.

In other words, *mahr* is a sum of money or other property promised by the husband to be paid or delivered to the wife in consideration of the marriage.

The other word generally used for *mahr* in the Holy Qur'an is *ajr*, meaning reward, a gift that is given to the bride. In fact, *ajr* is that in which there is gain but no loss. The word *sadaqa* is also used in the Holy Qur'an to indicate the nuptial gift. Another word used in the holy Qur'an to indicate the nuptial gift is *faridah* (4:4), literally what has been made obligatory or an appointed portion. The word *mahr* is also used in the Holy Qur'an to signify dowry, or the nuptial gift. According to the Holy Qur'an, the *mahr* is given as a free gift by the husband to the wife, at the time of contracting the marriage:

And give women their dowries as a free gift. (4:4)

The payment of the *mahr* on the part of the husband is an admission of his wife's independence, for she becomes the owner of the property immediately on her marriage, though before it, she may not have owned anything. The settling of a dowry on the woman at the time of marriage is obligatory:

**And lawful for you are all women besides these, provided that
you take them in marriage**

**not committing fornication.
Then as to those whom you profit by (through marriage), give
them their dowries as appointed.** (2:24)

In the case of a Muslim marrying a Christian or a Jewish woman,
the Qur'anic injunction is:

**And the chaste from among the believing women
and the chaste from among those
who have been given the Book before you,
when you have given them their dowries,
taking them in marriage.** (5:5)

It would appear from this that the Holy Qur'an makes the payment of *mahr* necessary for a valid marriage. The *ahadith* of the
Prophet also lead to the same conclusion.

Sayyiduna 'Umar, the second Khalif, and Qadi Shurayh have
decreed that[14] if a wife remits the whole of her *mahr* or part of it
but later on demands it back, her husband shall be compelled to pay
it because the very fact that she demands it is a clear proof that she
did not remit it of her own free will.

When is Mahr to be Paid?

The payment of *mahr* is necessary even though it might be a
very small sum.[15] In exceptional cases, marriage is legal even
though the amount of *mahr* has not been specified but it is obligatory and must be paid afterwards. Thus the Holy Qur'an says,
speaking of divorce:

**There is no blame on you
if you divorce women
when you have not touched them,
or appointed for them a dowry.** (2:236)

This shows that marriage is valid without specifying a dowry.
A *hadith* also speaks of the validity of a marriage, even though
dowry has not been named.[16] But the dowry must be paid, either at
the time of the consummation of the marriage or afterwards. The
amount of dowry in this case depends upon the circumstances of the
husband and the social position of the wife. The Holy Qur'an makes
this clear by requiring the provision for the wife to depend upon the

circumstances of the husband:

> ...the wealthy according to his means
> and the straightened in circumstances
> according to his means. (2:236)

In a *hadith* it is related that the case of a woman whose husband died before fixing a dowry and consummating marriage was referred to 'Abdullah ibn Mas'ud, who decided that she should be paid a dowry according to the dowry of women of like status to herself. This decision, which was accepted as a model by the jurists, meant that the reasonable amount for a dowry is dependent on the relative position in life and social status of the parties to the marriage and will differ from place to place, period to period, and country to country.

Thus it is clear that a dowry is an essential ingredient of Islamic marriage without which the contract is not complete. The *ayat* refers to the dowry as *sadaqah*. This has its own significance, since the word *sadaqah* also means charity. Thus it is implied that a dowry is to be given as a free gift which becomes the property of the wife. Therefore she has full authority to give any portion of her dowry to her husband or guardian. Another verse in the Holy Qur'an declares:

> But if you decide to take a wife
> in place of another,
> even if ye had given the latter
> a whole treasure for a dowry,
> take not the least bit of back.
> Would you take it by slander and
> a manifest wrong? (4:20)

This verse makes it clear that the dowry belongs to the divorced woman, whatever its value. The husband is not entitled to take it by force or threat or through slander. Every husband should fear Allah and have *taqwa* (piety) and refrain from usurping the rights of his former wife. The Qur'an further emphasises:

> And how could ye take it
> when ye have gone in unto each other,

This shows definitively that the dowry belongs to the woman and not to her former husband. So if he tries to get it back through foul means such as laying a calumny against her and slandering her, he earns the disapproval of the Holy Qur'an. In another verse, the Holy Qur'an declares:

> **And chaste women,**
> **except those whom your right hands possess**
> **(i.e. captives in a *jihad*).**
> **Thus hath Allah ordained (prohibitions) against you except for**
> **those all others are lawful,**
> **provided ye seek (them in marriage)**
> **with gifts from your property,**
> **desiring chastity, not lust.**
> **Seeing that ye derive benefit from them,**
> **give them their dowries**
> **at least as prescribed,**
> **but if, after a dowry is prescribed,**
> **ye agree mutually to vary it,**
> **there is no blame on you. (4:24)**

It means that a dowry is obligatory and without it no Muslim marriage can take place. It further shows that the dowry is a means of reward or remuneration. When a man takes a woman in marriage, she surrenders her person to him. So a man should also surrender some of his property to her. Of course the woman has a right to release her husband from the dowry or to change its amount after reaching a mutual understanding with him.

The Qur'an makes payment of the dowry obligatory not only in a marriage between Muslims but also in marriage of a Muslim to a woman who is a *kitabiyah* (belonging to the people of the Book, (i.e. Jews or Christians):

> **(Lawful unto you in marriage)**
> **are (not only) chaste women who are believers,**
> **but chaste women among the People of the Book,**
> **revealed before your time,**
> **when you give them their due dowers**
> **and desire chastity,**
> **not lewdness, nor secret intrigues (5:6)**

The Holy Qur'an also says:

**There is no blame on you
if ye divorce women before consummation
or the fixing of their dowry.
But bestow on them (a suitable gift).
The wealthy man according to his means,
and the poor according to his means.
A gift of a reasonable amount is due from those
who wish to do the right thing. (2:236)**

This shows that if a Muslim divorces his wife before the marriage is consummated or before the dowry is fixed, he is required to give a suitable amount to the divorced woman according to his own capacity. But if the *sadaq* is fixed before marriage and divorce takes place before the consummation of the marriage, he has to pay one-half of the fixed *sadaq* to her. (2:237)

No Fixed Amount for the Mahr

Looking at the *Shari'ah* of Islam does not fix any definite amount or thing of a definite value as a *mahr*. The injunctions of the Qur'an are silent on this issue. However there are *ahadith* on the subject:

It is narrated by 'Amir ibn Rabi'ah that a woman belonging to the Banu Fazarah was married with a pair of shoes as her *mahr*. The Messenger of Allah asked her, "Are you happy with a pair of shoes?" She replied that she was. The Prophet, may Allah bless him and grant him peace, then permitted her to marry.[17]

Likewise, a woman came to the Prophet and said, "Messenger of Allah, I wish to give myself to you." Then she stood for a long time waiting for an answer. Then a man stood up and said, "O Messenger of Allah, if you do not need her, let her marry me." The Prophet then asked him, "Do you possess anything you can give as *sadaq*?" He replied that he had only a pair of trousers which, if he gave them to her, would leave him without any. He was asked to give something even if he only had an iron ring. Since he had none, the Prophet asked, "Do you know anything from the Holy Qur'an?" He replied, "Yes", and named the *surahs* that he remembered. The Prophet then said, "I declare you two married with what you possess of the Qur'an."[18]

In this case, the chapters or portions of the Qur'an that the man remembered were considered as his *mahr*. But a *hadith* must be properly understood. It does not negate the minimum *mahr* fixed by Imam Abu Hanifah or Imam Malik. Ibn al-Qayyim explained this *hadith* to mean that the *mahr* is the right of a woman, and the pious lady mentioned in the above *hadith* was satisfied with the man who was at least knowledgable in the Qur'an:

"And this was dearer to her than property given by her husband, because *sadaq* in reality is meant for a woman to benefit her. If she was happy with the knowledge and Islam of her husband and his recitation of the Qur'an, then this was the best *mahr* and most beneficial to her."[19]

As for giving a large *mahr*, there is absolutely no harm in that. Once Khalif 'Umar said that the Prophet had declared that no-one should give a *mahr* larger than 400 dirhams. When he got down from the *mimbar*, a lady of Quraysh asked him, "Have you not heard the injunction of Allah? '*And you give one of them qintars.*' "

'Umar went back to the mimbar and declared: "I was advising you not to give more than 400 dirhams as *mahr*. Whosoever wishes may give as much property as he wishes to give."[20]

The husband, however, has no right to demand back any of the dowry given to the wife in consideration of the marriage or ornaments, clothes, etc., given to her as gifts. It is utterly against the moral principles of Islam to ask for the return of anything given to another as a present or gift. The Holy Prophet likens this disgraceful behaviour to a dog licking up its own vomit. It is very shameful on the part of the husband to keep back or demand after the divorce what he himself gave to his wife. As a matter of fact Islam exhorts the husband to give her something at her departure. (Qur'an, 2:229)

Other Conditions concerning the Mahr

The payment of the *mahr* should be in the form of something that has a value even though it may be small. According to the Hanafi school, the smallest amount possible for a *mahr* is 10 dirhams but according to Maliki schools the least *mahr* is equivalent to 3 dirhams. There is no fixed minimum in the Shafi'i and Hanbali schools nor among the Shi'ites. If someone gets married on the strength of a dowry consisting of a quantity of wine or pigs or anything that is unlawful in Islam and which cannot be owned or bought or sold by a Muslim, the marriage is null and void. All the jurists of the four schools agree upon this point. The Maliki school insists that half of the *mahr* should be given on the spot for the consummation of a valid marriage. *Mahr* can be given promptly on marriage or can be postponed until after the marriage. The Hanafi point of view is that the payment of the dowry can be delayed, either in part or in whole, but it must not be just forgotten completely.

The proposal for giving the *mahr* should not be made in an ambiguous way such as saying, "I marry you for £100 to be paid when the clouds come or when the sky produces rain or a traveller arrives," etc. The Malikis say that the *mahr* may be a definite thing like an animal known by sight or description or a particular kind of horse like an Arabian horse or it may be a definite amount of money as mentioned earlier.

Even if the dowry is not given on the spot, it should not be delayed through a flimsy promise like "to be postponed until death or our separation." According to the Shafi'i and Hanbali schools it is lawful if the entire *mahr* is paid later but it should not be forgotten completely. Once the amount of *mahr* is fixed and it is ready at hand, the payment should not be delayed. According to the Malikis, it may be given to the wife on the day of the marriage except when the woman herself wants to take it later. The *mahr* should not be postponed simply because the wife is sick. The Maliki school views that if it is fixed that half of the dower has to be paid straight away and half later on with the specific words that "I marry you on £50 to be paid now and the remaining £50 later on", it is necessary in this situation to pay her the full amount before consummation.

According to the Shafi'i school, the wife can refuse to allow consummation of the marriage by the husband if the *mahr*, once agreed to be paid completely, is not paid. If the husband did not pay the *mahr* or maintenance to the wife, the wife can take an action to annul the marriage. The Shafi'i jurists say that if the husband is unable to pay the *mahr*, as agreed, then it is up to the wife either to be patient or she may take the matter to the *Qadi* to annul the marriage.

No limits have been placed on the amount of *mahr*. The words used in the Holy Qur'an show that any amount of dowry may be settled on the wife:

And you have given one of them a heap of gold. (4:20)

Thus no maximum or minimum amount has been laid down. The Holy Prophet paid varying amounts to his wives. In one case when the Negus paid the amount to Umm Habiba (Abu Sufyan's daughter), who was then in Abyssinia where the marriage took place, it was four thousand dirhams, while in the case of the other wives it was generally five hundred dirhams. The *mahr* of his daughter Fatima was four hundred dirhams. The lowest amount mentioned in *ahadith* is, as we have already heard, an iron ring, and the man who could not procure even that was told to teach the Holy Qur'an to his wife.[22]

In some *ahadith* two handfuls of meal or dates are also mentioned. The amount of the dowry may however be increased or decreased by the mutual consent of the husband and wife at any time after marriage; and this is plainly laid down in the Qur'an (4:24). The wife is the owner of the *mahr* and hence she may remit the dower wholly or partially. The remission of the *mahr* in the terminology of *fiqh* is called *hibat al-mahr*.

In the Hanafi school, however, if the dower has been specified, then the question arises whether it is to be given promptly or it is to be deferred or delayed. *Mu'ajjal* or prompt *mahr* is to be paid immediately after marriage if demanded by the wife. It is agreed that if it is *mu'ajjal* or delayed or deferred, then it becomes payable on the dissolution of the marriage or if some ugly event takes place which disturbs the harmony of the family. When a *mahr* is fixed (*musamma*), it may be split into two equal parts and it may be stipulated that one part should be paid immediately on demand from the wife and the other part paid on the death of the husband or divorce or the happening of some special event.

Rights of Inheritance of Muslim Women

Qur'anic injunctions have made it clear that there is a share for men and a share for women in inheritance. This is because women and minor males were denied inheritance not only in pagan Arabia, but also in Biblical law.

According to Cheyne and Black's *Encyclopaedia Biblica*, "Women appear to have been universally and in every respect regarded as minors as far as rights of property went. Only sons, not daughters, still less wives, can inherit."[23] Looking at the Qur'anic injunctions, it becomes clear that "the male will have as much as the portion of two females." As Sir Muhammad Iqbal rightly remarked, this was not determined because of any inferiority inherent in her "but in view of her economic opportunities, and the place she occupies in the social structure of which she is part and parcel."[24]

He further says that while the daughter, according to Muslim Law, "is held to be the full owner of the property given to her both by her father and her husband at the time of marriage, while at the same time absolutely owning her dower money, which may be immediate or deferred according to her own choice and under the terms of which she can hold possession of the whole of her husband's property till payment is made, the responsibility of maintaining her throughout her life is wholly on her husband."

Apart from this, the Islamic Shari'ah has generally put greater economic responsibility on men while women's role economically is comparatively speaking much lighter.

However even so, if among the offspring of the deceased, the daughters are the only heirs, and they are more than two, they have two-thirds of the share. If there is only one daughter, she will have one-half.

All distribution, of course, takes place only after the legacies and debts, including funeral expenses, have been paid.

Shares Allotted to Mothers

If a father with children dies, his mother gets one-sixth as her share. She also receives one-sixth if her son has any brothers or sisters (full or half). However if there is only one brother or sister she receives a third. She also gets one-third of the residue when she is joint inheritor along with a man's father, wife or husband. After taking away the share of the husband or the wife from the rest of the estate, she will get one-third while the father takes the rest on the basis of the doctrine of *Umariyyatani*. When discussing this issue, it is essential for us to understand the *Umariyyatani* case.

The Umariyyatani Case

The case of the *Umariyyatani* occurred during the Khalifate of Sayyiduna 'Umar, the second Khalif, when he decided an inheritance case between a father, mother and husband, and again between a father, mother and wife.

The most important thing to note in this case is the share of a mother when there are:

(1) Mother, father and husband.

(2) Mother, father and wife.

In normal circumstances, we have seen that the share of the mother is either one- sixth of one-third of the total estate. But the case of *Umariyyatani* made the mother's share one-third of the residue after taking away the shares of the wife or the husband.

Father	Husband	Mother
Residue	1/2	1/3 of Residue

or

Father	Mother	Wife
Residue	1/3 of Residue	1/4

In normal circumstances, where there are father, mother and husband or wife, the shares would look like this:

Father	Husband	Mother	
Residue	1/2	1/3	
1	3	2	share divisions

or

Father	Mother	Wife	
Residue	1/3	1/4	
5	4	3	share divisions

When the first example is carefully examined, it can be seen that the share of the mother is more than the share of the father. As a normal rule where a female comes together with a male, the share of the male is double the share of the female as is the case of sons and daughters or brothers and sisters. Or the shares are equal as in the case of a father and mother when there are also children.

In the second example the normal rule again did not apply, because the mother's share is so near to the share of the father.

The majority of Muslim jurists say that the normal rule is not suitable for Muslims and that therefore the rule to be applied is that of the *Umariyyatani*. When the husband or wife have taken their share, whatever remains should be divided between the father and the mother. The mother takes one-third and the father takes the rest. Referring to the Qur'anic verse which says that if the father inherits, the mother will take one-third and the father one-third, they say that this is applied only where the two of them are sole joint-inheritors. But in the case where they inherit together with either a husband or a wife, the mother takes one-third of the residue.

Some *Sahabah* and jurists like Ibn 'Abbas, Da'ud az-Zahiri, Sayyiduna 'Ali, Mu'adh ibn Jabal and Qadi Shurayh are of the opinion that the Qur'anic rule must be left untouched. The Qur'an says that in the absence of children and brothers or sisters, the mother receives a quarter of the total estate. Therefore, the injunction must be applied as has been commanded.

Ibn Sirin agrees with Sayyiduna 'Umar regarding the first example where father comes with mother and husband, but he does not accept the second formula where the father comes with mother and wife because in that case, as he maintains, the father should get more than the mother. Therefore, the rule must be amended:

according to Ibn 'Abbas:

Father	Mother	Husband
Residue	1/3	1/2
2	4	6

or, according to *Umariyyatani:*

Father	Mother	Husband
Residue	1/3 of Residue	1/2
2	1	3

Shares Allotted to Children
1) Whatever the parents leave after their death, their children and nearest kin have the rights over their property which should be shared according to the guidance from the Qur'an.
2) The power of testamentary disposition extends over only one-third of the property; the remaining two-thirds are distributed among the heirs

Shares Allotted to Wives
The following shares are allotted according to the Qur'anic injunctions:
1) When the wife dies, the husband takes half of his deceased wife's

property if she leaves no children. The residuaries get the rest of the property.

2) If the deceased wife leaves a child, the husband gets only a quarter.

3) As we have seen before, the female share is generally half of the male share. The widow, therefore, gets a quarter of her deceased husband's property, if he leaves no children.

4) If he leaves children, the widow gets only one-eighth.

5) If the widows are more than one, their collective share is a quarter if there are no children. But if there are children, their collective share is one-eighth which they share equally between them. (The Bible was less kind to the widow as it did not place her among the husband's heirs. In Judaism, the Jewish widow is a charge on her children or, if she has no children, she depends on her own family.)

6) The golden rule of inheritance still remains the same. That all distribution will only take place after legacies and debts, including the funeral expenses are already paid.

Husbands receive half of the estate of their deceased wife in the absence of any sons and daughters. In the event that there are sons or daughters, or grandsons or granddaughters, he only gets a quarter.

Husbands and wives inherit from each other subject to the following two conditions:

1) The contract of their marriage should be a valid one. What is essential for the purpose of *mirath* is not the consummation of the marriage, but the actual contract of marriage. Any woman claiming the *mirath* has to prove the validity of her marriage in accordance with either the Maliki school or any of the other Sunni schools. According to the Maliki school, if a marriage is contracted during a final illness, neither of the spouses is allowed to inherit after the death of one or the other of them. However, some jurists say that if the contract is with the agreement of the other heirs the widow is allowed to inherit. The other schools say that the marriage must have been solemnized in accordance with their own schools only.

2) The surviving spouse has to prove that he or she is still married at the time of death, either in fact or by law, meaning that they are living together or in the case of a woman who has been divorced, that she is still serving her *'iddah* period and that the divorce is revocable (*raji'*). If the divorce took place during the final illness of the husband, she is allowed to inherit, on the presumption that her

husband might have divorced her in order to prevent her from her right of inheritance.

The Maliki school takes an altogether different view . They say that the woman inherits whether the divorce is revocable or not, or whether the husband intended to prevent her from her right of inheritance or not, whether she is serving her *'iddah* period or has finished her *'iddah*. If she has married another husband, she will still be allowed to inherit from her first husband if he dies due to sickness. A husband will not not inherit from his wife if she dies in this way.

According to the Zahiri school, if the divorce is final the wife is not allowed to inherit, even if it is proved that the husband divorced her intentionally to prevent her from her right of inheritance.

The Shafi'i school partly agrees with the Zahiri school and partly with the Hanafis on this issue, saying that a wife is entitled to inherit from her husband if she is still serving her *'iddah* period.

The Hanafi school holds that she inherits even if she has finished her *'iddah* provided that she has not remarried.

If the divorce was at the woman's request or due to compulsion, then the accusation cannot be made that it was in order to prevent her from her right of inheritance *(mirath)*. It is interesting to note that Sayyiduna 'Uthman gave inheritance to the wife of 'Abdu'r-Rahman ibn 'Awf, and Sayyiduna 'Ali gave it to the wife of 'Uthman.

Shares Allotted to Daughters

The daughter, if she is the sole daughter and there are no sons inheriting from the father, will receive the residue. But if there are two or more daughters, they will receive two-thirds between them in the absence of a son. If there are daughters and sons, they share the residue with the sons taking twice the share of the daughters.

Shares Allotted to Full Sisters

If there is only one full sister, she inherits half in the absence of an heir i.e. children, father, or grandfather and full brother.

If there are two or more full sisters, they share two-thirds in the absence of any heir.

If they have any full brothers the inheritance is divided according of the Qur'anic principle :

To the male a portion equal to that of two females.(4:11)

Female Inheritance in General

It will be seen from the brief look at this subject above that the whole business of inheritance in Islam is one of considerable complexity. The various possible permutations of relationship are almost innumerable and it is clearly beyond the scope of general work such as this to go into all the details. However the important point to be made is that female relatives both ascendant and descendant have automatic rights of inheritance when the necessary conditions apply.

Grandmothers, mothers, aunts, sisters (both full and half), daughters and granddaughters all have rights of inheritance under Islamic law thus granting to them as women a legal and economic status which was not achieved by their counterparts under European and other legal systems until very recently.

The details of the exact shares and how and when they apply can be gained from books of *fiqh* on the subject and from *'ulama*, some of whom have made the subject of inheritance their speciality.

11

FEMINISM IN MUSLIM COUNTRIES

Feminism which began as a movement for the emancipation of women is certainly not of recent origin. The word was first coined by the younger Dumas in a pamphlet, *L'Homme-Femme*, which he wrote in 1872.[1] In 1792, Mary Wollstonecraft published her book, *The Rights of Women*, in which she emphasised the need for the betterment of the lot of women and ridiculed the accepted notion of double morality in the Western World, for men and women. During the days of European imperialism and the scramble to take over the Muslim world, the influence of feminism spread into Muslim countries.

The first victims of the glittering Western way of life were the Muslim rulers of various Muslim countries. In the days of the political decline of Islam, they were made to believe that the Muslim world was lagging behind because of the "maltreatment and slavery of women".

The Feminist Movement in Egypt

In Egypt, the leaders of this movement were rulers like Muhammad 'Ali and Isma'il Pasha. The so-called social and cultural "reforms" initiated by these rulers compelled the Egyptians to abandon their traditional Islamic outlook and way of life. Muhammad 'Ali Pasha reconstructed the educational system in Egypt on the French model and sent several members of the ruling family to be educated in European universities.[2] The *'ulama'* and the Egyptian Muslims were not happy about it but, as Professor Gibb puts it, "...slowly and grudgingly and at times unconsciously the conservative opposition was forced to yield point by point, and each fresh (worldly) advantage gained, spurred 'the reformers' to further efforts. It is significant that it was only in Egypt that a movement for social reform crystalized out, and that around this the problem of women's freedom emerged. Nothing can show more clearly how deeply westernization had struck roots, and how radically it was transforming the outlook of the intellectual leaders of

Egypt."[3]

The other factor which encouraged the feminist movement was the influence of Christian missionaries.

In 1826, Muhammad 'Ali sent the first batch of Egyptian students to different universities in the West. The first group consisted of 44 different students, but by the year 1833, the number had increased to 114.[4] Similarly students from Turkey, Syria and other parts of the Muslim world had also started visiting different Western centres of learning in various parts of Europe. These students, both male and female, were completely imbued with foreign ideas and started to dislike the traditional outlook of their own people. It was a purely natural consequence, as Professor Gibb says, since, "...no intelligent student could spend three or four years in a European capital, in daily intercourse with its people, reading their literature, good and bad, without imbibing something more than the mere externals of Western civilization." [5]

Muhammad 'Ali Pasha was so much enamoured of European education that he wrote a letter to Jeremy Bentham, the famous English radical thinker, in which he sought his advice regarding the education of his heir-apparent.

His successor, Khedive Ismail Pasha (1830-1895) who ruled between 1863 and 1879 initiated a definite move for the 'freedom' of women. He had been educated at Paris and wanted Egypt to attain the same cultural level as the Europeans. So during his reign, he established schools which increased in number from 185 to 4,817 all of which put emphasis on a European style of uniform and European syllabi.

He particularly encouraged the unveiling of women and in 1873 founded in Cairo the first school for Muslim girls under the patronage of his wife. By 1875 there were already 298 female students in the school.[6]

At around the close of the 19th century, there appeared four eminent writers who in their zeal for launching reformist programmes wrote about the elevation of the status of women. Their writings helped to built the ideological foundations of the feminist movement in Egypt which ultimately resulted in what is found in Egypt today. They were: Jamal ad-Din al-Afghani, Shaykh Muhammad 'Abduh, Qasim Amin, and Malak Hifni Nasif.

Jamal ad-Din al-Afghani (1839-1879) was a great revolutionary whose influence spread in the Muslim world during the 19th century. Although he came from Afghanistan, he became the leader of reformist movements all over the Muslim world, especially in Turkey, Egypt and Iran.

In Egypt, however, his personality left a lasting impression. During his short stay he created a group of enthusiastic Egyptian followers. Professor Charles Adams portrays in his book, *Islam and Modernism in Egypt*, the popularity and achievements of Jamal ad-Din al-Afghani in these words:

"When the news of his arrival became known, he was besieged in his lodging by eager students to whom he expounded some of the most advanced textbooks on theology, philosophy, jurisprudence, astronomy and mysticism with a view to raising up a generation of young writers who could ably set forth in print the new ideas which he was imparting." [7]

His pupil Shaykh Muhammad 'Abduh carried his mission further. Referring to the social reforms of Muhammad 'Abduh, Adams says:

"One of the prominent and essential ideas in the pages of Muhammad 'Abduh's writings and in *Al-Manar* is the necessity for the training and education of girls, no less than of boys, and for the reform of the social conditions and customs affecting the lives of the women of Muslim lands. In nothing does Islam show its fitness to be considered a modern world religion, they held, more than in the high position of honour which it accords to women. In all essential respects according to its teachings, she is on an equality with man." [8] He repudiated the practice of polygamy in Egypt.

Thus during the later half of the 19th century the teachings and writings of these renowned scholars paved the way for "modernism" in the Arab world. Their efforts were concentrated on freeing Islam from so-called rigid orthodoxy. Al-Afghani firmly believed that in all essentials, Islam was thoroughly capable, by virtue of its closeness to human nature, of adapting itself to the changing conditions of every age. His ideas were fully shared by his pupil, Muhammad 'Abduh, who has been unanimously acclaimed as "one of the creators of Modern Egypt." The initial impulse to 'reform' given by these scholars increased manifold with the beginning of the 20th century, and in every Muslim country the number of 'reformers' increased.[9] The work done by Kamal Ataturk in Turkey, Sa'd Zaghlul in Egypt and Reza Shah in Iran was based on this new interpretation made by these scholars. In their zeal for modernism, these rulers acted in an un-Islamic fashion.

Qasim Amin followed in the footsteps of the early Egyptian 'reformers'. He wrote two of his revolutionary books pertaining to women. Mawlana 'Abdul-Hasan 'Ali Nadwi has given an excellent exposition as to how some of our Muslim leaders, and even *'ulama'* have fallen prey to Western propaganda and have called for the "emancipation of women".[10]

An unmistakeable proof of the social and cultural impact made by the West on the Egyptian mind is found in the writings of Qasim Amin, a front-rank leader of the movement for the freedom of women in his country, more especially in his books entitled *Tahrir al-Mara'at* (Women's Freedom) and *Al-Mara'at al-Jadida* (Modern Woman). In *Tahrir al-Mara'at*, Qasim Amin advances the claim that "there is nothing in the abolition of *purdah* which may be opposed to the teachings of Islam," and then goes on to say: "The Islamic Shari'ah is merely the name of a few fundamental truths and general checks and restraints. Had its function been to go into the details of law it would have ceased to be a universal legal system for all people and all times. The injunctions of the Shari'ah which are based upon current usage and contemporary issues can be amended according to the needs and circumstances of the time, what it insists upon simply is that the amendments do not violate the general foundations enunciated by it."[11]

The discussion in the book centres around four topics: *purdah*, the active participation of woman in different walks of life, polygamy, and divorce. On all these issues the author has adopted a Western standpoint regarding Islam. He has also given a wrong interpretation of the word Shari'ah and all that it stands for in his book, *Tahrir al-Mara'at*.

Qasim Amin's westward-looking mentality is more noticeable in his other book, *Al-Mara'at al-Jadida*. In it he has adopted the Western style of reasoning which rejects all truths and convictions that are not realisable through experience, even though they may be based on religion. This is what Westerners describe as the "scientific method". In the end, Qasim Amin makes a strong case for emulating Western social and cultural norms and traditions. He castigates the Egyptians for glorifying the past and taking pride in their old culture and civilisation.

"This is our real ailment which needs to be eradicated first of all. The only way to get rid of it is that we should make our younger generations acquainted more and more with Western civilization and its conditions and circumstances so that in due course (which is not going to be a long drawn-out time, in any case), the reality may unveil itself before them like the blazing sun. We will realise the value and importance of Western civilization and see for ourselves that no reform is possible unless it is based on modern Western knowledge and that all human affairs, whether moral or material, must be subservient to the dictates of reason and learning.

"That is why we find that all the civilized communities of modern times, however different they may be in race, language, nationality and religion, are very much similar to each other in matters of political organization, government and administration, family structure, education, language, script and architecture, and even in such minor things as dress, modes of greeting, food or drink. For this very reason we project the people of the West as a symbol of perfection, insist on their veneration as an ideal, and appeal to our countrymen to study the position and status of the Western woman." 12

These two books attained great popularity in the progressive section of Egyptian society and thanks to them, a strong urge was created among the Egyptian women for equality and emancipation and for discarding *purdah*. Mixed gatherings of men and women became commonplace and Egyptian women and girl students began to freely undertake voyages to Europe and America. Writes Professor Mohammad Hussain:

"Religious-minded Muslims were greatly perturbed over the trend of freedom and immodesty the movement had bred among women. They objected vigorously to the revolution that was taking place in women's lives. They were against the growing intolerance of the authority of father and husband and of other established customs and practices and looked with dismay at the unprecedented haste with which women were discarding the loose and modest Egyptian dresses in favour of the tight and short European ones."13

Qasim Amin's teachings aroused the feelings of Egyptian women who demanded more freedoms and rights.

Malak Hifni Nasif was one of the women collaborators of Qasim Amin. She was the daughter of Hifni Bey Nasif, who was a distinguished member of 'Abduh's group, and was given a liberal education. She joined the Saniyyah Training School for Women Teachers in 1893 and after completing her studies, taught in various Government schools. She referred to herself as *"Bahithat al-*

Badiyah" which means "The inquiring desert woman." She died on October 17, 1918.[14] Her articles and talks show that she wanted to revolutionize the position of Egyptian women in all spheres of life.

Arslan Bohdanowicz says: "Less than ten years after the publication of Qasim Amin's books, his ideas had spread so widely that even the conservative circles ceased to deny the necessity of education for women."[15]

The foundation of the Egyptian University in 1909 was another landmark in the history of the feminist movement in Egypt. Special lectures were arranged for women lecturers. The first lecturer was a French woman, but in 1911 Madam Labiba Hashim, editor of the most popular woman's paper, *Fatat ash-Sharq* (The Eastern Girl), was asked to deliver a series of lectures on education. In 1912, two other Muslim women were invited to deliver a course of lectures on some other subjects.[16]

It was during this period, also, that leadership of the feminist movement passed into the hands of Huda Sha'rawi (d. September 1947). Her father, the speaker of the Legislative Assembly, and her husband, a member, were among the foremost men who were struggling for the independence of Egypt. This high social status also enabled her to exercise great influence.

She started her career as a leader of the movement in 1919 when she became the chairman of the women's Executive Committee of the Wafd party. Unveiling and the wearing of European dress in Egypt is attributed to her efforts because there was no official move for unveiling in the country before that.[17] In 1923, for the first time, on the eve of the International Feminist Congress in Rome, she formed an Egyptian Feminist Union from the members of the Wafdist Women's Executive Committee. She, with two other women leaders, left for Italy to participate in this Congress. All of them were unveiled and in European dress. After her return from the Congress, she intensified her propaganda of the feminist movement and then started a monthly review, *L'Egyptienne*[18]. In March 1927 a charity show was organised in Cairo in which the feminist leaders came unveiled and in European dresses and later that practice became general.[19]

The next step the feminist movement took was the reform of the marriage law. For the achievement of this purpose, a commission of jurists and scholars was appointed by the government in 1927. This commission made recommendations with regard to 'reforms' in

Marriage and Divorce.

On the 11th of March 1928, a new Marriage and Divorce Law was promulgated. Then the number of women's organizations and associations increased swiftly, for instance the Girl Guide Movement was started in 1929 under the leadership of Munira Sabri. The popularity of this organization can be imagined from the fact that by the year 1948, the figure of membership had reached fourteen thousand.

The impact of Western culture, the Western way of life and, above all, Western education was so deep in some Muslim countries like Egypt that even the *'ulama'*, the "successors of the Prophet"[20] became the champions of the feminist movement.

Without any disrespect for Shaykh Jamal ad-Din al-Afghani and his pupil, Shaykh Muhammad 'Abduh, I would like to appeal to Muslim scholars the world over to re-examine the role they played in this most difficult period of Islamic history when the Christian West had almost dominated the Muslim world. I have a feeling that perhaps they went too far in proposing reforms in the Shari'ah. Perhaps with the best of intentions, they proposed so-called 'reforms' in the matter of Shari'ah and galloped on the unbridled horse of reason and imagination, giving *fatawa* (juristic opinions) which did great damage which they did not live long enough to see.

Shaykh Rifa'ah at-Tahtawi was another of the "reformers". A contemporary of Shaykh 'Abduh, he was one of the first batch of Al-Azhar students selected by the Egyptian rulers to go for higher education in France and was supported by his contemporary scholars. On his return, At-Tahtawi became a very influential man in Egypt and made it his mission to preach European thought in Egypt.[21] He wrote a book called *The Honest Guide for Girls and Boys* which was published in Cairo in 1873 and which teaches Egyptian women to imitate Western women. Qasim Amin was also a contemporary of Shaykh 'Abduh, who was a living witness to all these feminist and modernist activities. It is very possible that these writers were inspired by his teachings. Shaykh 'Abduh died in Cairo in 1905 .

Many of my Egyptian friends will not be happy to read that not only did Egypt shelve, and to a great extent discard, the Islamic system of values as taught by the Qur'an and the Sunnah by adopting Western culture and the Western way of life, but it also exported it to other Arab and Muslim countries. Walking in the streets of many cities in Egypt, one feels that one is in Europe. Women with short skirts and tight Western dresses are to be seen everywhere and night-clubs and dance halls can be seen in most streets. There is no prohibition on wine-drinking. The "belly dance" is in many ways an innovation of Egypt. All this, unfortunately, is endorsed even by some of the *'ulama'* of Al-Azhar, the ancient seat of Islamic learning in Cairo.

The Feminist Movement in Turkey

In Turkey, the sponsors of the Tanzimat Movement initiated so-called reforms in the name of modernism. In her book entitled *Turkey Faces West*, Halide Edibe discusses the efforts of the Tanzimat leaders in the following words:

"For one of the new ideals it (Tanzimat) wanted to introduce was a better position for women. The greatest poet and dramatist of the school, 'Abdul Hak Hamid brought women heroines into his classical plays. "The progress of a nation is measured by the status of its women" became a general saying." [22]

Later on traditional Islamic classical education, which meant the learning of Persian and Arabic for the higher classes of Turkish women was replaced through the efforts of the Tanzimatists by a new westernized form of education for women. French now became a compulsory subject in the curriculum of girls' education.[23] Although the Tanzimat movement did not last long, its evil influence remained long after people had completely forgotten its leaders.

In the year 1876, another attempt was made to initiate political and social reforms in Turkey. By now, strong propaganda in favour of the so-called reforms had been created, and the upper classes who had been steeped in the western form of education were everywhere determined to undo the traditional Islamic systems which they blamed for the maladministration of the past. In the year in question a group of westernized Turks under the leadership of Midhat Pasha came to the helm of affairs and decided to formulate a new constitution. It was then that the feminist movement once again gained popularity among the masses.

Western ideas of liberty and freedom for women caught the imagination if not of the entire population then at least that of the aristocracy. Female education became a topic of public discussion. G.F. Abbot confirms this in his book, *Turkey in Transition:*

"The middle of last century formed an ephemeral embodiment in Midhat Pasha's constitution of 1876 and a more striking expression in the July Revolution. From Midhat Pasha's time, Turkish families of rank began to employ European governesses for the education of their daughters. A craving for Western culture invaded the harem."[24]

It was during this period that Ziya Gokalp's influence came into the limelight. Ziya's father was also a victim of pro-western propaganda. He wanted his son to acquire Western education even at the cost of losing his religion. He said to one of his friends regarding the education of his son:

"I must send Ziya to Europe to become learned."

"If he goes to Europe, he will become an infidel," replied his friend. To this Ziya's father answered,

"If he stays here, he will become an ass." [25]

This shows how the people of the Muslim world were unduly impressed by the educational superiority of the West and this in itself was quite an important factor in their inferiority complex when comparing themselves with the social and cultural advancement of the people of the West.

As a sociologist, Ziya was not qualified to write or juristic opinions, but still he made up his mind to reinterpret Muslim law in favour of women, and put down arguments which could counteract the influence of the circles of the *'ulama'* of Turkey. He made a so-called fresh interpretation of the Shari'ah and distinguished between divine elements and social elements in the Shari'ah. In his view social elements rested not on textual revelation, but on *'urf*, which in juristic terminology means customary law. In his opinion family law was under the domain of customary law which could be modified by the collective will of the community.[26] Basing his thesis on the wrong premises, Ziya drafted his suggestions for 'reforms' on behalf of political leaders. He also started a weekly journal called *New Review*, in which he published a series of articles in support of his new but misguided thesis.

In one of his articles he wrote: "The subjugation of women, which has gone so far as to deprive them of their most elementary rights and freedoms, is not of Turkish or Muhammadan origin. It is an unfortunate heritage passed on to us by Persians and Byzantines and the Turkish and Muhammadan beginnings were in fact, feministic in character." [27]

He wrote another pamphlet in which he attacked the institution of *purdah*. In his opinion nothing was so injurious to social progress as this custom, which he thought led to the utter humiliation of women in every sphere of life. The thoughts expressed in this pamphlet are so radical that it could not be given general publicity at that time. It was secretly printed and privately circulated. It contained the following anti-Islamic statement:

"The forms of social life have nothing to do with religion, whose field is the world to come and those problems which as yet reason cannot solve. A social usage such as veiling is easily traceable to certain instincts and to primitive social origins. Its perpetuation in the present century is the greatest possible insult to our women. It is based on the supposition that they are fundamentally immoral and must constantly be kept by physical barriers from taking wrong steps. An ethical system which is based on external guardianship, and not on confidence in character and self-respect, is not worthy of the Turkish nation. The discarding of veils can have no immoral consequences and will be on the contrary the starting point of a higher ethical development." [28]

After the end of the war, the practice of bringing women into men's society became more and more common and popular. In 1918, a revised family law was passed in favour of women, and Islamic courts headed by the *Shaykh al-Islam* were placed under the authority of the Minister of Justice, enabling women to make use of the revised family law. In view of the services of women during the war, these reforms were considered to be insufficient. The feminist leaders continued their work, and after the war and the establishment of the Turkish Republic in 1923, Kamal Ataturk became their greatest champion. He formulated new schemes and policies for the modernisation of Turkey and made the emancipation of women his first and foremost concern.

In her book, *Turkey Old and New*, Selma Ekrem, a modern woman Turkish writer, has given an account of Ataturk's interest in the cause of women:

"Kamal Ataturk realised that the country needed free, educated women if it was ever to assimilate the changes he had in mind. Women must assume their rights. He toured the country again, urging women to throw off the veil to take part in national affairs and step into their rightful place. He said in one of his speeches that no country could advance with half of society free and other half lacking all freedom." [29]

The Feminist Movement in Iran

The feminist movement also spread to other parts of the Middle East. Iran was certainly not left out. In the 19th century, Tahira, popularly known as *Qurratu'l-'Ayn*, which means coolness or consolation of the eyes, or *Zarrin Taj*, which signifies Golden Crown, became one of the leaders of the Baha'i religious movement in Iran which was started by Muhammad 'Ali Bab in the mid-nineteenth century.

She was born in 1820 and after being imprisoned, was put to death in August 1852 when she was thirty-two years old. She was the first Iranian woman to throw off the veil and put on European dress and addressed large gatherings of men in public meetings. Western writers have praised her a great deal, although in Iran she is considered to be a devilish woman who corrupted the morals of Iranian women and confused their religious beliefs by preaching the Baha'i faith.

Martha L. Root in her book, *Tahira, the Pure, Iran's Greatest Woman*, says about her:

"Viewed in this light, one can understand her chaste spirit, her matchless courage, not only in the danger to her life but in her being the first woman in the Eastern Muslim World to dare to lay aside the veil even in brief moments, and in being courageous enough to go to the Badasht conference to consult with the group of men followers of the Bab." [30]

Lord Curzon had also paid tribute to her in the following words:

"Beauty and the female sex also lent their consecration to the new creed (Baha'ism), and the heroism of the lovely but ill-fated poetess of Qazvin, *Zarrin Taj* (crown of gold) or *Qurrat-ul-'Ayn* (solace of the eyes), who throwing off the veil, carried the missionary torch far and wide, is one of the most affecting episodes in modern history." [31]

The feminist movement in Iran, therefore, started with the Baha'i movement. The principles enunciated by the Bab were and are favourable to women. Later on, Sadigeh Khanum Daulatabade and Khanum Azamodeh, whose names are closely associated with female education in Iran, became the pioneers in this field. The work of the these two enthusiastic women was welcomed everywhere in the country and education of girls became a common phenomenon.

A boost to the morale of the feminists was given by Reza Shah who founded a new dynasty when the old Qajar dynasty collapsed after the First World War. The new ruler, who had risen from the minor position of a military official by sheer luck, tried to follow in the footsteps of his contemporary, Kamal Ataturk in Turkey. Under him, in 1925, the first Iranian woman was given special permission by the Foreign Minister to leave for Paris to be educated. She was detained on the frontiers by the ever-watchful police until a telegram authorizing her departure was sent by the Shah.[32]

In 1926, there was already a move to throw away the *chador*, or Iranian veil. In January, 1936, the Shah appeared at the Teheran High School to present the diplomas for the year. He was accompanied by the Queen and his two eldest daughters. They were all unveiled and were wearing short European dresses. On this occasion he made a special speech, some relevant sentences of which are quoted in Elwell Sutton's book, *Modern Iran*:

"I am extremely pleased to see women who, as the result of knowledge and study, have come to know their true position and to understand their rights and privileges. As Madame Tarbiat has pointed out, the women of your country because of their exclusion from society, have been unable to display their talent and ability."

He concluded his speech with the remarks, "I expect from you educated women, now that you are conscious of your rights and privileges, that you are going to perform your duty towards your country."

12
EPILOGUE

The end of each decennial span in the modern world has brought a variety of innovations in pornography, fashions, television shows, use of women in advertisements, night clubs, operas, disco bars and theatres, etc., which all go to put a distinctive stamp on the period. As we enter the 'gay nineties' in yet another decade, we ask how the nineties are going to be different from the eighties as far as women are concerned? What name should they bear? I think the 'gay nineties' are perhaps going to turn out to be a period of yet more disgrace and degradation for womanhood as a whole.

To a great extent, the way we perceive a decade is affected and influenced by the period which immediately precedes it. The sixties and seventies appear pale when you think of the so-called 'progress' in women's 'liberation' and 'emancipation' in the eighties. Like the decennial spans, the centuries are also affected by the preceding centuries. Will Durant, an eminent European scholar, has tried to connect the past centuries with the present in his study of the position of women in twelfth and thirteenth century Europe and has gone even as far as suggesting that medieval Europe and medieval Christendom were apparently as prolific as our own irreligious age in licentiousness, profanity and fraud.

In order to show very clearly how past centuries affect the present - how women were misused in the Middle Ages and how that legacy has continued into our time - this Christian scholar has made a factual study of the position of women in medieval times in his book, *The Age of Faith*.. Discussing the moral vices prevalent in the Middle Ages of the Christian era, Will Durant says:

"In all classes men and women were hearty and sensual; their festivals were feasts of drinking, gambling, dancing, and sexual relaxation; their jokes were of a candor hardly rivalled today; their speech was freer, their oaths vaster and more numerous. Hardly a man in France, says Joinville, could open his mouth without mentioning the Devil."

Let us compare this situation with what obtains at present in

Western countries and even in those Muslim countries which have adopted the Western way of life. The situation today is not so different from the medieval period. The only difference perhaps that one notices is in the new methods and devices of these rampant malpractices which we have invented in our times.

As happens in the Western world today "...by the age of sixteen the medieval youth had probably sampled a variety of sexual experiences." Henry, Abbot of Clairvaux, wrote about France that "ancient Sodom is springing up from her ashes." The Penitentials, ecclesiastical manuals prescribing penances for sins, mention the usual enormities, including bestiality; an astonishing number of beasts received such attention. Cases of incest were numerous.

Premarital and extramarital relations were apparently as widespread as at any time between antiquity and the twentieth century. Rape was common. Knights who served highborn dames or damoiselles for a kiss or a touch of the hand might console themselves with the lady's maids; some ladies could not sleep with a good conscience until they had arranged this courtesy. The Knight of La Tour-Landry says, if we are to believe him, that some men of his class fornicatecd in church, "nay on the altar"; and he tells of "two queens which in Lent, on Holy Thursday, took their foul delight and pleasure within the church during divine service." William of Malmesbury described the Norman nobility as "given over to gluttony and lechery", and exchanging concubines with one another "lest fidelity should dull the edge of husbandry". Illegitimate children littered Christendom, and gave plots to a thousand tales. The heroes of several medieval sagas were bastards - Cuchulain, Arthur, Gawain, Roland, William the Conqueror, and many a knight in Froissart's Chronicles.

The only difference today is that sex is taught in the schools as a subject, and many girls have sexual experience at the age of twelve or before.

Homosexuality is openly practised and is legalized in many countries. Prostitution which has spread almost everywhere is not a new phenomenon but it has adjusted itself to the times. Some women, in the Middle Ages, while on pilgrimage, according to Bishop Boniface:

"Earned their passage by selling themselves in the towns on their route. Every army is followed by another army, as dangerous as the enemy."

"The Crusaders," reports Alber of Aiz, "had in their ranks a crowd of women wearing the habit of men, they travelled together without distinction of sex, trusting to the chances of a frightful promiscuity."

University students, particularly in Paris, developed urgent or imitative needs, and girls established centres of accommodation to provide for them. In Rome, according to Bishop Durand II of Mende (1311), there were brothels near the Vatican, and the Pope's marshals permitted them for a consideration. The Church showed a humane spirit toward prostitutes. A council at Rouen in the eighth century, invited women who had secretly borne children to deposit them at the door of the church, which would undertake to provide for them; such children were brought up as serfs on ecclesiastical properties. Although penalties for adultery were severe - Saxon law, for example, condemned the unfaithful wife to lose her nose and ears, and empowered her husband to kill her - adultery was common not withstanding.

Today there is no longer even a pretence of penalising adultery. A prostitute can openly solicit her clients and *zina* is committed with impunity and without any attempt at concealment, the only condition being mutual consent between the participants. It is only *zina bi'l-jabr* (rape) which is considered an offence. The Middle Ages is described as a profligate age. "Medieval Christian society," said the learned and judicious Thomas Wright, "was immoral and licentious." Present day Western society is even more so.

Today the checks on public morality have become weak and are considered unnecessary, and, as a result, a flood of sexual licentiousness, nudity and promiscuity has burst in on the West. Theatres have becomes the scenes of moral perversions and nude performances; dwelling places are decorated with nude and immoral paintings; and prostitution has become so widespread and popular that fashionable areas of Soho in London, Champs d'Elysées in Paris and Manhattan in New York have become centres for visitors from various parts of the world who are entertained in the striptease clubs were live sex performances are given. The modern world has become replete with immoral and immodest themes with the result that no literary work devoid of such themes can become popular with the common people or intelligentsia.

There is also a rapid disintegration of families. Divorce is not regarded as at all shameful, so much so that some women calculate their age by the number of husbands they have had. Some men and women even swap their wives and husbands. It reminds us of the early Christian period when Juvenal (60 - 130 AD) wrote about a woman who went through eight husbands in five years. St. Jerome (340 - 420 AD) made mention of a wonderful woman whose last husband was the 23rd in succession, and she was herself the 21st wife of her husband. What is happening now is merely a repeat of the early Christian era in which the Church fathers had to take the drastic and extreme step of preaching celibacy as the official creed of the Church.

In this study, we have seen that the difference in objectives between the Western and Islamic ways of life necessarily leads to a fundamental difference between the methods of social organization adopted by Islam and Western civilization. The aim of Islam is to establish a social order that segregates the spheres activity of the male and the female, discourages and controls the free intermingling of the sexes, and curbs all such factors as are likely to upset and jeopardize social discipline.

On the other hand, the objectives of Western civilization requires that both sexes should be drawn into the same field of life and activity, that all hindrances and impediments should be removed if they are likely to obstruct their free and promiscuous intermingling, and that they should be afforded unlimited opportunities to enjoy each other's beauty and physical charms. This situation has naturally posed a great challenge to healthy family life and has endangered the very institution of marriage.

The contribution of modern Western writers to this falling standard of morality is enormous. Paul Adam in his book, *Le Morale de l'Amour*, had censured youth for committing the folly of making their sweethearts believe that they are passionately in love with them and cannot live without them. All he is asking them to do is to be natural and have sex with the opposite sex like animals do without any trace of attachment. Otherwise, the passionate relationship might lead to the bond of marriage.

Other modern writers have also supported the abolition of the age-old institution of marriage and have thus led the younger generation down the path of destruction. Says Paul Bureau, "I have not changed my opinion, I have not made peace with society, and marriage is always, according to my judgement, one of the most barbarous institutions ever imagined. I have no doubt that it will be abolished if the human race makes any progress towards justice and reason; a bond more human and not less sacred will replace it, and will secure the existence of offspring who will be born of a man and a woman, without ever fettering the liberty of either. But men are too gross and women to cowardly to demand a noble law other than that which rules them; heavy chains must bind beings who lack conscience and virtue." With such destructive teachings, naturally, a Western home cannot be a commendable home for woman. Marriage has become just a lottery.

Heart-breaking transference of love and affection, neglected wives, forsaken children, mistresses, and street girls are common features of Western life. Western women are the most unhappy creatures on earth and their position in society has created innumerable social, psychological and moral problems that they are desperately trying to solve or at least to alleviate, but all in vain.

It is against this background that we must view the noble and natural Islamic conception of woman's equality to man in her free will, nature, spiritual responsibility and ability to raise herself to high planes of virtue, consciousness of Allah (*taqwa*) and honour, as stressed in many verses of the Holy Qur'an, as well as many *ahadith* of the Prophet. Equality between the sexes, therefore, is an established Islamic fact, although this equality does not mean that she is identical with man. Allah gave man and woman different physiques because He intended them to perform different roles.

To man and woman, Allah assigns an equal share of mutual and spiritual responsibilities and it is in this sense that a Muslim man and woman are equal. The modernists call on Muslim women to strive for equality with men, but their call is devoid of significance because Muslim women have already had this equality for fourteen centuries now, given to them by Allah, the Most High. The modernist call is misleading and can only appeal to those who are ignorant of what their religion offers them.

However, the family as any other sound social institution, should entrust its leadership to that one of its members who is best able to shoulder this responsibility. It is in this light that the following verse should be understood:

"Women have rights similar to those of men in kindness and
men have a degree above them.
Allah Almighty is Wise." (16:72)

The word 'degree' haas been fully explained before. It does not mean man's absolute superiority as a human being, but it signifies a certain functional advantage which imposes extra duties on him. Man is physically strong and consequently, he is charged with the responsibility of maintenance, protection and leadership. Motherhood, looking after children, and keeping the house where rest, comfort and compassion is provided by her to every member of the family, constitute sufficient burden for the woman. Therefore, it is the man's responsibility to earn, maintain and provide for the family's necessities and the woman is relieved of such financial and economic responsibilities in the Shari'ah even if she is wealthy.

The honour and integrity of a woman is mentioned, as we have seen, in many verses of the Qur'an and the *ahadith* of the Prophet and hence the Qur'an prescribes very severe punishment for those who falsely accuse chaste and pure women of sexual immorality. (24:4) This is to arrest unhealthy and irresponsible propaganda by unscrupulous men against chaste women and keep society free from scandals. Islam also stopped and forbade the hateful female infanticide which used to be practised by the pagan Arabs thus preserving the female life and dignity. Female children should be received with gratitude and joy as boons from Allah to be loved and cherished.

We have also observed that the highest regard and consideration is given to motherhood. The Prophet said, "Paradise lies under the mother's feet." And the Qur'an recommends good treatment and kindness to the mother for "...she carries the child with strain upon strain" (14:31) and because she nursed him when he was a helpless infant. A man's obligation towards his mother is far greater than his obligation to his father according to the teachings of the Holy Prophet (peace be upon him).

Likewise, we have also observed that women are encouraged to study and acquire learning. All women and men are alike in this regard. Both should acquire education "from the cradle to the grave". In short, Islam has made adequate provision for preparing women as equal partners of men.

But the educated Muslim youth in Arab and other Muslim countries, as well as in non-Islamic states, are falling easy prey to an inferiority complex. They are prone to the ideas of misguided Western philosophers, psychologists, sociologists and economists. Freudian theories which have subsequently been rejected by many of the latest Western psychologists and philosophers are being accepted by so many Muslims without any analysis of the validity of these theories using the touchstone of the Qur'an and the Sunnah of the Prophet.

Maryam Jameelah, formerly a Jewish American lady and now a devout Muslimah, who has rendered a great service in enlightening the Muslim masses through her writings, gave the following message to Muslim women in Pakistan:

"What is most urgently needed in all Muslim communities is for all intelligent, capable, energetic and sincere sisters in faith to organize an effective and active Islamic movement for women and to enlist their children in the same. Efforts of individual mothers to give their children training in the Islamic ways, however praiseworthy, are woefully inadequate (today) to confront the dreadful evils, right outside the doors of even the most pious homes.

"I think the primary concern of all Muslim mothers who want a renaissance of the Islamic order is to enlist their children in the movement. How can we expect our children to grow up to love Islam when everything they learn at school and outside the home teaches them to revolt against all we stand for? If we tender excuses and more excuses that we are too busy with our housework and family and personal problems to do this and just let matters drift we can expect our adolescent sons and daughters to be interested only in fashions, cinema, pop singers, cabaret entertainers and sports events.

"Our children will do these things not because they are innately bad but because that is what their environment teaches them if we have nothing better to offer. To combat this evil, women who sincerely want an Islamic renaissance must first and foremost band together and collaborate in establishing their own Islamic primary schools to give our children the most thorough instruction we can in Qur'an, the traditions of the Holy Prophet (S.A.W.), the lives of Muslim heroes of the past and present and the rudiments of the Arabic language.

"They should also be taught *Wudhu* and *Salat* not only merely the ritual but much more important, its meaning in a loving and interesting manner. Since at the outset, classes could be held at home and Islamic textbooks are cheap in this country, this would not involve any great expenditure of money but would require intelligent organization, time, energy and resourcefulness. How many

Pakistani mothers have I seen who devotedly recite their *Salat* and conscientiously perform all their religious duties yet fail utterly to teach their children to do so.

"The greatest defect of observant Muslims today is that they recite Holy Qur'an merely as a ritual without understanding what they are reading rather than regarding the sacred book as a practical manual of everyday conduct to be acted upon. If Muslims were taught to understand and above all, translate into action, what they recite, the world would experience a veritable revolution which would put all previous revolutions to shame."

While speaking about the role of modern Muslim women in reconstructing a healthy Islamic society, Maryam Jameelah further suggests the following:

"Since the primary responsibility for the rearing of children falls upon the mother, upon her rests the responsibility for the moral, spiritual and character training of future generations. Islamic education for women and the young girls who will be future mothers is imperative, and illiteracy and ignorance should be combatted vigorously by providing separate schools and colleges for girls. Adult Islamic education for women must also be carried on by the Islamic movements. No Islamic movement can succeed if it neglects the proper education and training and discipline of girls and young women.

"Ignorant and illiterate mothers cannot possibily rear their children and raise them to be good, effective, capable and intelligent Muslims, in the world today." ("Maryam Jameelah Answers Questions, *The Criterion*, p. 46)

Summary of Qur'anic Guidance for Muslim Men and Women

To conclude we shall summarise the opening verses of *Surah al-Mu'minun*, the Qur'anic guidance to show Muslim men and women how to achieve real success and prosperity and provide them with a key to salvation from sorrow and evil and enable them to achieve their final goal. The seven brilliant jewels of a *mu'min's* faith (*iman*) as mentioned in these verses are:

(1) Humility
(2) Avoidance of vanity
(3) Charity
(4) Sexual purity

(5) Fidelity to trusts

(6) Fidelity to covenants

(7) An earnest desire to get closer to Allah

> **The believers must (eventually) win through;**
> **those who humble themselves in their prayers;**
> **who avoid vain talk;**
> **who are active in deeds of charity;**
> **who abstain from sex except with those**
> **joined to them in the marriage bond;**
> **or (the captives) which their right hands possess,**
> **for (in their case) they are free from blame,**
> **but those whose desires exceed those limits**
> **are transgressors;**
> **those who faithfully observe**
> **their trusts and their covenants;**
> **and who (strictly) guard their prayers;**
> **these will be the heirs, who will inherit Paradise;**
> **they will dwell therein forever. (23:1-11)**

A Muslim man or woman's guarding against every kind of sexual abuse or sexual perversion is included in the overall plan, outlined above, for his or her spiritual and worldly prosperity (*falah*). Humility in regular prayer will help to guard from every kind of evil and shameful thing (*fahsha' wa'l-munkar*). Deeds of charity will help to create love and mercy for mankind, thus preventing people from taking undue advantage of others, and will help to reduce greed and temptation and purify one's means of livelihood. Avoiding vanity in their actions and behaviour will help people to be more humble. Guarding against illicit sex, sexual abuse and sexual perversion will help build a healthy society.

The new psychology associated with the name of Freud traces many of our hidden motives to sex, and it is common knowledge that our refinement or degradation may be measured by the hidding workings of our sexual instincts. Self-control and control over one's carnal desire is an important requirement for spiritual elevation. This is the reason why the punishment for adultery (*zina*) is very severe and provides a good deterrent to keep people away from committing this crime which is corruptive of individuals, society and humanity at large.

This is also the reason why, as we have observed, the law of Islam makes marriage and divorce very easy, so that there may be less temptation for adultery or fornication.

Finally and most importantly it leads to both men and women having greater self respect and having genuine respect for one another. This, which is stressed again and again both by Allah in the Qur'an and by the Prophet in words and actions, may Allah bless him and grant him peace, is the key to a healthy human society.

NOTES

Notes for Preface

1. Carrel, Alexis, *Man and the Unknown,* quoted in *Spectrum, Yaqeen International,* vol. 28, no. 24, Apr. 22 1980, p.275.
2. Ibid.
3. Abu Saud, Muhammad, *Sex Roles, a Muslim Point of View, Al-Ittihad,* vol. 15, no. 3, July 1978, p. 14.
4. Ibid.
5. Weitz, Shirley, *Sex Roles,* New York, Oxford Univ. Press, 1977, p. 42.
6. Lynn, D.B., *The Father, His Role in Child Development,* Monterey Books, California, 1974, pp. 14-21.
7.Weitz, Shirley, *Sex Roles,* New York, Oxford Univ. Press, 1977, p. 42.
8. Diamond M.A., *A Critical Evaluation of the Ontogeny of Human Sexual Behaviour, Quarterly Review of Biology,* 40 (1965).
9. Carrel, Alexis, *Man and the Unknown,* op. cit., pp.84-87.
10. Ludovici, Anthony, M., quoted in *Spectrum, Yaqeen International,* vol. 28, Apr. 28, 1980.

Notes for Chapter 1

1. Nazhat Afza, *The Position of Woman in Islam,* Karachi, 1968, p. 11.

Notes for Chapter 2

1. 'Abduh, Muhammad, *Tafsir al-Manar,* p. 68 et seq.
2. cf. 'Abd-al-'Ati, Hammudah, *The Family Structure in Islam,* Indianapolis, American Trust Publications, 1977, pp. 172 - 173.
3. See Al-Albani, Muhammad Nasiruddin, *Hijab al-Mar'at al-Muslimah fil Kitab wal Sunnah.,* Third edition, Beirut, 1389 A.H.
4. Maududi, Abul A'la, *Purdah and the Status of Women,* pp. 186-187.
5. Ibid, pp. 181-182.
6. Ibid, pp. 179-180.
7. Al-Jassas, Abu Bakr, *Ahkam al-Qur'an,* vol. 3, p. 443.
8. Maududi, A.A., *Purdah,* op. cit., p. 192.

9. Al-'Aqqad, 'Abbas Mahmud, *Al-Mar'at fil-Qur'an*, Beirut, Third edition, 1969, p. 92.
10. Ibid.

NOTES for Chapter 3

1. See Qur'an 30:21 and 31:10; 50:7; 26:7; 2:25; 4:57; 4:1.
2. *Mawahib al-Jalil,* vol. II, pp. 403-404.
3. Al-Jaziri, 'Abdur Rahman, *Kitab al-Fiqh 'ala Madhahib al-'Arab'ah,* vol. IV, p. 4, Cairo, 1970.
4. Ibid, p. 5.
5. Ibid.
6. cf. *Hashiyah al-Dasuqi,* vol. 2, p. 215.
7. *Mawahib al-Jalil,* vol. III, pp. 405.
8. *Hashiyah al-Dasuqi,* vol. 2, p. 215.
9. cf. Ibn Asakir in his book *Kitab Ashal al-Mawwawik,* vol. II, p. 68.
10. *Al-Jami' li-Ahkam al-Qur'an,* vol. 3, p. 67, also cf. Sayyid Sabiq, *Fiqh as-Sunnah,* vol. 6, Kuwait, 1968, p. 206.
11. cf. Sayyiud Sabiq, *Fiqh as-Sunnah.*
12. *Kitab al-Fiqh 'ala Madhahib al-'Arba'ah,* op. cit., 4, p. 76.
13. Ibn Kathir, *Tafsir Ibn Kathir,* for further details see Yusuf Ali, *The Holy Qur'an,* 3, note 76.

NOTES for Chapter 4

1. Cf. Sayyed Sabiq, Fiqh as-Sunnah, op. cit., vol. 6, p. 223.
2. Imam Malik, al-Muwatta', ed. Muhammad Fu'ad al-Baqi, Kitab al Saib, Cairo (undated).   3. Cf. Coulson, A History of Islamic Law, Edinburgh, 1971, 1, p. 208.
4. Ingells, N.W., Biology of Sex, quoted by Khalid Rashid, op. cit., p. 72.
5. Proceedings of the C.M.S., 1857, p. 32; also World Missionary Conference, 1910, p. 11.
6. Parrinder, Religion in an African City, O.U.P., 1953, p. 166.
7. Ibid, pp. 166-167.
8. Trimingham, J.S., Islam in West Africa, O.U.P., 1959, p. 163.
9. I.H. van Driesen in his investigation into the Economics of Peasant Agriculture in Ife Division (for the Ife Project) has provided us with the following examples: (1) A Yoruba Muslim, living in

Ijugbe, owning a considerable area of land and with an estimated monthly income of 60 pounds, aged 55, has taken only one wife; (2) another Muslim of Asabi with an annual income of 60 pounds is monogamous.

10. J.B. Webster, The African Churches among the Yoruba 1888-1922, Clarendon Press, 1964, p. 84.

11. An Alfa is a Yoruba Muslim teacher and preacher. It is an equivalent of "Mallam" in Hausa which is a corrupt form of the Arabic word Mu'allam.

12.. G.A. Olawoyin, The System of Customary Marriage among the Ifes, a paper read at a Seminar of the Institute of African Studies, University of Ife, 1967/68, 7, p.2.

13. Arshad Masood, "Muslims less Polygamous than Non-Muslims", Radiance, January 15 1978. I am grateful to Mr. Arshad Masood for giving me permission to use the data collected by him in this article.

14. Even Ha-ezer, 1:9; also cf. Klein, Isaac, A Guide to Jewish Religious Practice, New York, 1979, p. 388.

15. Ibid, p. 389.

16. see Khurshid Ahmad, The Position of Woman in Islam, op. cit., p. 28.

17. Besant, Annie, The Life and Teachings of Muhammad, Madras, 1932, pp. 25-26.

18. cf. Khurshid Ahmad, op. cit., pp. 28-29.

19. Galwash, Ahmad, The Religion of Islam, vol. 1 (undated), p. 44, "Muslim Home", by H.H. Nawab Sultan Jahan Begum Sahiba, Ruler of Bhopal, India.

20. Encyclopaedia of Modern Knowledge, vol. 5, p. 2572.

21. Quoted from "Sex, Life and Faith" in C.N. Ahmed Moulavi's Religion of Islam: A Comprehensive Study, Calicut, 1979, pp. 304-305.

22. Nazhat Afza, The Position of Women in Islam, Karachi, 1969, p, 10

.23. "Maryam Jameelah Answers Questions," The Criterion, vol. 13, No. 1 & 2 January-February 1978, pp. 45-46.

24. Lemu, B. 'A'isha, Woman in Islam, London, 1976, pp. 27-29.25. Miftah Dar as-Sa'adah, p. 629; Zad al-Ma'ad, Vol. 4, p. 66.26. See Fatawa of Shari'ah by Shaikh Shaltut of al-Azhar, p. 424, p. 454.

27. cf. Time Magazine, November 3, 1980, p. 58.28. Time Magazine, "The Bishops and Birth Control, November 3, 1980, p. 58.

NOTES for Chapter 5

1. *Kashf al-Khala'*, vol. 2, 302. Also *Tafsir al-Qurtubi*, vol. 1, p. 318.
2. Al-Ghazali, *Ihya' 'Ulum id-Din*.
3. Sayyid Sabiq, *Fiqh as-Sunnah*, op. cit., vol. 8, p. 59.
4. To understand the rule of arbitrators in detail, see Abu Zahrab, Muhammad, *Al-Ahwal al-Shakhsiyyah*, Cairo, pp. 277-278.
5. See *Sharh al-Kabir*, vol. 8, also cf. Al-Sabuni 'Abd al-Rahman, *Hurriyat al-Zawjain fi'l-Talaq*, Cairo, 1968, pp. 85-86.
6. *Mughni al-Muhtaj*, vol. 3, p. 307.
7. Ad-Dardir, *Sharh Mukhtasar Khalil*, vol. 2, p. 423.
8. Pallem and Wynne, New Catholic Dictionary, New York.
9. Bauer, Woman and Love, p. 291.
10. Geddes and Thomson, p. 259.
11. Havelock Ellis, Man and Woman, p. 288
12. Ibid, pp. 289-290.
13. Ibid, p. 291.
14. Bauer, Woman and Love, p. 173.
15. cf. Kisch, Sexual Life of Women, p. 173.
16. *Hashiyah ad-Dasuqi*, vol. 2, p. 406.
17. *Nihayah al-Muhtaj*, vol. 6, p. 47.
18. Al-Sabuni, *Hurriyah al-Zawajain fil Talaq*, op. cit., p. 595.
19. The commentators of the Qur'an have also derived the rule in respect of *khul'* from other injunctions contained in the Holy Qur'an, 4:20; 4:128; 4: 130.
20. Ibn al-'Arabi, *Ahkam al-Qur'an*, 1, 194. See also *Tafsir al-Qurtubi*, 3/145.
21. *Al-Mudawwamah al-Kubra*, 5, 22; also *Tafsir al-Qurtabi*, 3/138.
22. Al-Shaukani, *Fath al-Qadir*, 1, 213.
23. Ibid, 1, 214; See also *Al-Mughni*, 8, 174.
24. Al-Baihaqi, *Al-Sunnah al-Kubra*, 7, 376.
25. *Fath al-Bari*, 9, 346.
26. *Hashiyah ad-Dasuqi*, vol. 2, p. 406.
27. Ibn Kathir, vol. 1, p. 267.
28. *Bidayah al-Mujtahid*, 2: 40; *Al-Mudawwamah al-Kubra*, 5, 28.

Here the words *Mukhtali'ah* and *Muftadiyah* are discussed by Imam Malik.
29. *Bahr al-Ra'iq,* 4/80.
30. See also *Taj al-Madhhab,* 2/291.
31. *Al-Mughni,* 8, 215.
32. *Hurriyah al-Zawajain* , 2/557; see also *Al-Insaf,* 8/389.
33. Ibid, p. 559.
34. *Bahr al-Ra'iq,* 4/97.
35. *Al-Muntazai' al-Mukhtar,* 2/435.
36.*Al-Mabsut,* 6/180; cf. *Bahr al-Ra'iq,* 4/180.
37. *Mukhtasar an-Nafi',* p. 227; see *Jawahar al-Kalam,* 5/ 3/ 360.
38. *Sharh al-Nil,* 3/556.
39. *Mukhtasar al-Quduri,* 2/23.
40. *Hashiyat Ibn Abdin,* 2/428.
41. *Mukhtasar al-Muzni,* 4/51.
42. *Sharh al-Kharshi,* 3/169.
43. *Al-Mughni,* 8, 174.
44. Sayyid Sabiq, *Fiqh al-Sunnah,* op. cit., vol. 8, p. 177.
45. This is the opinion of Ibn 'Abbas and 'Ali. See Shawkani, *Nayl al-Awtar,* vol. VI, pp. 306-307.
46. Al-Shafi'i, *Risalah,* op. cit., p. 168.
47. See Malik, Vol. II, pp. 589-90, Abu Da'ud, Vol. II, p. 293, al-Shafi'i, *Kitab al-Umm,* Vol. II, pp. 205-206; Shawkani, *Nayl al-Awtar,* Vol. VI, p. 305.

NOTES for Chapter 7

1. *Miftah Dar as-Sa'adah,* p. 629; *Zad al-Ma'ad,* Vol. 4, p. 66.
2. Abdur'Rauf, Muhammad, *The Islamic View of Women,* New York, 1977, p. 125.
3. See *Fatawa of Shari'ah* by Shaikh Shaltut of al-Azhar, p. 424, p. 454.

NOTES for Chapter 8

1. Al-Bayhaqi, *As-Sunan al-Kubra,* vol. 8, p. 208.
2. *Nail al-Awtar,* vol. 7, p. 160; see also Al-Bukhari, Muslim, at-Tirmidhi and Abu Da'ud.
3. Al-Jassas, *Ahkam al-Qur'an,* p. 162.

4. Al-Bayhaqi, *As-Sunan al-Kubra*, vol. 8, p. 8.
5. Abu Da'ud, *Kitab ad-Diyat*; see also an-Nisa'i.
6. At-Timirdhi.
7. As-Suyuti, *al-Ashaya wa'n-Nazair*, p. 228.
8. Al-Mawardi, *al-Ahkam as-Sultaniyyah*, p. 22.
9. Ibn Hazm, *al-Muhalla*, vol. 1, p. 509.
10. Al-Mawardi, op. cit., p. 35.
11. Ibid, p. 77.
12. Ibid, p. 241.
13. See Ibn Hazm, *al-Fasl*, vol. 4, p. 166; also at-Taftazani, *al-'Aqa'id an-Nasafiyah*, p. 185.
14. Al-Bukhari, vol. 9, p. 70, for details see *Al-Ahkam as-Sultaniyyah*, p. 27
15. at-Taftazani, *Sharh as-Sa'd 'ala al-Maqasid*, vol. 2, p. 2777.
16. Al-Baghdadi, *al-Farq bayn al-Farq*, pp. 89-90.
17. Ibn Hazm, *al-Fasl*, vol. 4, p. 167.
18. Al-Mawardi, *al-Ahkam*, p. 27.
19. See al-Mawardi, op. cit., p. 65; *Fath al-Qadir*, vol. 5.
20. Al-Mawardi, p. 64.

NOTES for Chapter 9

1. *Al-'Iqd al-Farid*, vol. 1, p. 276.
2. Ibn al-Hajj, *Al-Mudkhal*, vol. 2, p. 277.
3. See *Fatawa Qadi Khan*, published with *Fatawa Alamgiriyah*, vol. 1, p. 443.
4. *Tadhkirah al-Huffaz*, vol. 1, p. 27.
5. At-Tirmidhi, *Abwab al-Manaqib*; al-Hakam, *al-Mustadrak*, vol. 4, p. 443.
6. Ibn Hajar, *Fath al-Bari*, vol. vii, pp. 82-83.
7. Ahmad ibn Hanbal, *Musnad*, vol. 6, p. 337.
8. *Tahdhib al-Asma' wa's-Sifat*, vol. 2, p. 349.
9. Ibn Hajar, *Tahdhib at-Tahdhib*, vol. 12, p. 56, and see also Ahmad ibn Hanbal, *Musnad Ahmad*, vol. 6, p. 323.
10. Ibn Hajar, *Tahdhib at-Tahdhib*, vol. 12, p. 444.
11. An-Nawawi, *Taghib al-Asma' wa's-Sifat*, vol. w, p. 364.
12. Ibn Khallikan, *Wafayat al-A'yan*, vol. 2, p. 169.
13. Ibn Habban, *Tahdhib at-Tahdhib*, vol. 8, p. 353.
14. *Al-Isti'ab fi Asma' al-As-hab*, Tadhkarah Zaynab bint Salmah.
15. Al-Bukhari, *Kitab al-Ahkam*.

16. Ibn al-Barr, *Al-Isti'ab fi Asma' al-As-hab*, Tadhkirah Umm ad-Darda'.
17. *Tahdhib al-Asma' wa's-Sifat*, vol. 2, p. 360.
18. *Tahdhib al-Asma' wa's-Sifat*, vol. 2, p. 353.
19. *Tahdhib al-Asma' wa's-Sifat*, vol. 2, p. 363.
20. *Newsweek*, March 17, 1980, p. 50.

NOTES for Chapter 10

1. Abu Saud, Muhammad, "Sex Roles - A Muslim Point of View, *Al-Ittihad,* vol 15., no. 3, July, 1978.
2. See Toynbee, A.J. in his article in *World Review*, March, 1949.
3. Abu Saud, Muhammad, "Sex Roles - A Muslim Point of View, *Al-Ittihad,* vol 15., no. 3, July, 1978, p. 27.
4. Abu Da'ud, *Kitab at-Talaq.*
5. Al-Bukhari, *Kitab Tafsir Surat al-Ahzab*; also *Musnad Ahmad,* vol. 6, p. 56.
6. See al-Bukhari, *Kitab al-Jum'ah.*
7. Ibn Sa'ad, *Tabaqat Ibn Sa'd,* vol. 8, p. 228.
8. Ibid, vol. 8, p. 220.
9. Ibid, vol. 8, p. 212.
10. Ibid.
11. *Newsweek*, March 17, 1980, p. 49.
12. Sullivan, *Alcoholism*, quoted in *Spectrum Yadqeen International*, vol. 28, no. 24, April 22, 1980, p. 275.
13. Scott, George, Ryley, *A History of Prostitution*, quoted by Khurshid Ahmad, *The Position of Woman in Islam*, Karachi, 1969, pp 35-36
14. Sayyid Sabiq, *Fiqh as-Sunnah*, vol, 7, p. 58.
15. Al-Bukhari, ch, 678, *hadiths* 51 and 52.
16. Abu Da'ud, ch. 12, *hadith* 31.
17. Narrated by Ahmad, Ibn Majah and at-Tirmidhi.
18. Al-Bukhari and Muslim.
19. Quoted by Sayyid Sabiq, *Fiqh as-Sunnah*, vol, 7, p. 63.
20. Narrated by Sa'id ibn Mansur and Abu Ya'la.
211. Abu Da'ud, ch. 12, *hadith* 28.
22. Al-Bukhari, ch. 67, *hadith* 52.
23. Ibid, ch. 67, *hadith* 51.
24. Cheyne and Black, *Encyclopaedia Biblica*, 4 vols, Black, London, cc. 2724, 2728.
25. Iqbal, Dr. Muhammad, *Reconstruction of Religious Thoughts in*

Islam, Lahore, pp. 236-237.
26. Letournean, *Evolution of Marriage*, pp. 259-269.

NOTES for Chapter 11

1. *Encyclopaedia Americana*, 1947 edition, vol. 11, p. 107.
2. Bay, Rifa'at, *Awakening in Modern Egypt*, London, 1947, p. 90.
3. Gibb, H.A.R., *Whither Islam*, London, 1932, p. 64.
4. Bay, Rifa'at, *Awakening in Modern Egypt*, London, p. 41. '
5. Gibb, op. cit., p. 48.
6. cf. Bohdanowicz, Arslan, "The Feminist Movement in Egypt", *Islamic View*, August, 1951, p. 26.
7. Adams, C.C., *Islam and Modernism in Egypt*, London, 1933, pp. 6-7.
8. Ibid, p. 230.
9. Ibid, p. 2.
10. Nadwi, Abu'l-Hasan 'Ali, *Western Civilisation, Islam and Muslims*, Lucknow, 1974, pp. 100-102.
11. Amin, Qasim, *Tahrir al-Mara'at*, Cairo, 1899, p. 169.
12. Amin, Qasim, *Al-Mara'at al-Jadida*, Cairo, 1900, pp. 180-182.
13. Mohammad Husain, *Al-Ittijahah al-Wataniyyah fi adab al-Mu'asir*, Cairo (undated).
14. Adams, op. cit., pp. 235-6.
15. *Islamic Review*, August, 1951, p. 27.
16. Ibid.
17. Ramadan, Abdel Meguid, Development of the Feminist Movement in Egypt, *Egypt Cultural Bulletin*, Dec. 1949, p. 9
18. Zaki, I., "The Emancipation of Egyptian Women", *Islamic Review*, February, 1949, p. 9.
19. Bohdanowicz, Arslan, op. cit., p. 28.
20. Hadith of the Prophet. The Prophet has said, "The learned of my *Ummah* are the successors of the Prophets."
21. 'Abdu'l-Ra'uf, Muhammad, *The Islamic View of Women and the Family*, New York, 1977, p. 142.
22. Edibe Halide, *Turkey Faces West*, London, 1930, pp. 84-85.
23. Ibid, p. 85.
24. Abbot, G.F., *Turkey in Transition*, pp. 24-25.
25. Benhar, Enver, Filozof Gokalp, 16, quoted in Ward, Barbara, *Turkey*, London, 1942, p. 27.
26. Gibb, H.A.R., *Modern Trends in Islam*, Chicago, 1945, p. 91.

27. Emin Ahmad, *Turkey in the World War*, London, 1930, p. 234.

28. Emin, op. cit., pp. 234-235, New York, 1947.

29. Ekram, Selam, *Turkey Old and New*, New York, 1947, pp. 80-81.

30. Root, M.K., *Tahira, the Pure, Iran's Greatest Woman*, n.d., p.3.

31. Curzon, *Persia and the Persian Question*, quoted in Martha Root's, *Tahira, the Pure, Iran's Greatest Woman*, pp. 80-81.

32. Ruth Frances, Woodsmail, *Muslim Woman Enter a New World*, p. 146.